MANY ARE CALLED

but most leave their
phone off the hook

MANY ARE CALLED

but most leave their phone off the hook

Exploring the Serious, Curious, and Hilarious Sides of Church

DOUG PETERSON

Illustrations by Dan Pegoda

ZondervanPublishingHouse
Grand Rapids, Michigan

A Division of HarperCollinsPublishers

Many Are Called
Copyright © 1992 by Doug Peterson
Requests for information should be addressed to:
Zondervan Publishing House
Grand Rapids, Michigan 49530   3/93

Library of Congress Cataloging-in-Publication Data

Peterson, Doug.
    Many are called, but most leave their phone off the hook : exploring
the serious, curious, and hilarious sides of church / by Doug Peterson.
       p.   cm.
    ISBN 0-310-57431-5
    1. Church development, New—Humor. 2. Church management—
Humor. 3. Christianity—Humor. 4. American wit and humor. I. Title.
BV652.24.P48 1992
250′.207—dc20   92-8646
                                       CIP

Edited by Julie Ackerman Link
Cover design by Jeff Sharpton
Interior design by Blue Water Ink

Printed in the United States of America

92 93 94 95 96 97 / CH / 10 9 8 7 6 5 4 3 2 1

This edition is printed on acid-free paper and meets the American National Standards Institute Z39.48 standard.

Booksto

To Mom and Dad,
With Love

God created the world in six days and rested on
the seventh. This was his way of demonstrating
that being a parent is even tougher than molding
a universe. It takes parents nine months to create
a newborn baby, and they don't get a day of rest
until eighteen years later.

Thank you for your love and hard work. And
thank you for creating a world that I treasure.
Thank you for creating our family.

CONTENTS

IN THE BEGINNING

"The hinge of history is on the door of a Bethlehem stable."
RALPH W. SOCKMAN

Our tale of the church begins when Jesus, while still a newborn, faced something most of us never face during all our years on earth. People wanted to kill him.

To be precise, one crazed, suspicious, paranoid king wanted Jesus dead. You know his name. Herod.

Herod has a long-standing reputation as the ultimate villain, and rightly so. But like most real-life villains, his heart wasn't completely petrified. When people were suffering, Herod sometimes decided not to collect taxes. Bible scholar William Barclay reports that in the year 25 B.C., Herod even melted down his own gold plate so he could buy food for starving people.

But that was only part of the picture. Herod was also incredibly jealous, and he despised the idea of anyone taking his throne. That's why he assassinated his three sons, Antipater, Alexander, and Aristobulus. He also did in his wife, Mariamne, and his mother-in-law, Alexandra.

With a record like that, it's no surprise that Herod was without friends. When he died, nobody would shed a tear. And he knew it. So he had made special arrangements to guarantee that someone would. According to Barclay, Herod left orders that when he died his soldiers were to round up a group of well-known citizens, frame them for some concocted crime, and then kill them. That way, Herod assured himself

9

that *somebody* would shed tears after his death—even if the tears weren't for him.

This is true. This is history. And so is the escape from Herod by Joseph, Mary, and their baby, Jesus. Several legends have sprung up around their escape to Egypt, and one of them—a children's story—has a message for adults as well. Here is my rendition of the tale.

The Spider's Gift

King Herod hated to look at the night sky. Every time he looked up he saw the large, bright star which reminded him that a new king had been born. It made him wish he could reach out and slap that star from the sky.

There could only be one king in the land. Herod knew this. That's why he had disposed of his three sons, whom he feared would steal his throne. Now, he was preparing to dispose of the Son of God.

Soldiers were already moving throughout the land, looking for the child, and making use of their swords.

But they underestimated the power of God. In a dream, God warned Joseph that Herod was out to kill Jesus. So Joseph gathered his small family and fled for Egypt. This was not a new strategy. Jews often fled to Egypt when they were being persecuted.

Travel was hard. And dangerous. And painful. And long. When night came across the land, Joseph and Mary, with their baby, hadn't reached Egypt yet. So they sought refuge in a familiar location—a cave. To Jesus it must have felt like coming home. He had been born in a cave.

The night was cold, but the breeze was mercifully soft.

To keep his donkey out of the sight of soldiers, Joseph hauled the animal into the cave. Even the stubborn donkey didn't complain about being moved into shelter on a frosty night.

Mary slept next to Jesus, keeping him warm with the heat of her body, while Joseph watched for trouble. The landscape was quiet. When the urge to sleep overcame him, Joseph slid deeper into the cave and joined his wife and child.

But not everyone had gone to sleep for the night. In the dark, a spider moved. Dropping a dragline from the top of the cave entrance, the spider dangled in space and watched the sleeping family. The spider, who went by the name of Lydia, knew she was in the presence of a king. Lydia also knew that she had to do something to keep Jesus warm.

Spiders do not have much cold-weather gear at their disposal—just three pairs of spinnerets that shoot silk from the backs of their bodies. Spinning silk was about the only task Lydia knew how to do well. So she decided to spin an orb-shaped web in the entrance of the cave. It wouldn't be much of a barrier to the cold—just a porous pattern of threads. But it was the finest gift she had to offer.

Lydia began with the bridge line, one single strand along the top of the cave's entrance. Then she quickly created five more foundation lines—the outer strands of the web. This was followed by a series of threads radiating from the outer foundation lines into the center. In the middle she constructed the hub, the bull's-eye of the web. Even though she was working at a furious pace, the web was turning out to be one of the cleanest, most skillfully produced of her short life. It was also the largest. In fact, it may have been the largest web ever created by a spider. Lydia raced around and around the web, firing silk from her spinnerets, creating a spiralling design.

When dawn broke, her creation was complete. Satisfied, Lydia looked at her masterpiece, white with the morning frost, and then scurried to find a place to sleep.

Sleep didn't last long. Lydia woke to a startling noise.

Horses. Men. Armor. Swords banging. The sound of soldiers.

Joseph and Mary heard the sound too. They roused themselves quickly and stared silently at the cave's entrance. Their child slept on. Fortunately, so did the donkey.

Joseph heard the horses come to a stop. Men dismounted. They were talking about the cave.

Joseph motioned for Mary to take the child and move farther into the cave until they were out of sight. But they could only go so far. If the soldiers took even a few steps inside, they would discover the family.

Mary prayed, Joseph prayed, and Jesus continued to sleep, as soundly as he would someday sleep in the middle of a storm.

The spider crouched. Lydia wished her fangs contained enough poison to stun a human. Then she could swing on her dragline like an eight-legged acrobat, drop onto the neck of the soldier in command, and sink her fangs into his skin.

"We have orders to check the area thoroughly," came one voice.

"Oh come on," said another. "I'm tired. Can't we look for the child from horseback? I haven't the energy to keep getting off my horse, on my horse, off my horse, on my horse all day long. We've been awake all night."

"We have orders. We *will* check this cave."

"Okay, okay. But next time, let's look from atop our horses."

Joseph wondered whether the soldiers could see their footprints outside. Or smell their donkey. Or smell *them,* for that matter.

Shadows filled the front of the cave. The footsteps stopped abruptly. There was a long moment of silence.

"Will you look at that?" said the voice belonging to the tired soldier.

"Just a spider web," said the other, dismissing it as nothing impressive.

"Listen," came the tired soldier's voice. "If there's a spider web in the entrance, nobody is inside. Nobody has been in this cave for ages! Let's stop wasting our energy."

There was another long silence. The soldiers took a few shuffling steps here and there. Joseph wondered what they were up to. But the spider knew. From her vantage point, Lydia could see that both soldiers were leaning over, looking closely at the web with its frosty coating.

"That's a big web," sighed the tired soldier. "Can you believe it?"

A third long silence. Deep in the cave, Jesus began to stir and Joseph became alarmed. This was not a good time for the child to wake up with a lung-full of crying. Joseph closed his eyes and braced himself for the sound of squalling.

"You're right," conceded the soldier in charge. "The web's unbroken. Nobody's been here."

The soldiers took a final glance at the spider web, mounted their horses, took a breath of morning air, and moved on, disappearing into the wilderness.

In the corner, beside his mother and father, the King of Creation was waking up with the rising sun. But the only ones who heard his cry were his parents and the donkey. Lydia was sleeping soundly.

✳   ✳   ✳

This book is not about spiders and spider webs. It is about the church. But I am convinced that the church and spider webs have a lot in common.

For example, spider webs, though flimsy, are made of a substance that is inherently stronger than steel. In the same way, an individual church is a fragile institution, susceptible to division and quarreling. But the universal church is everlasting, for it is woven out of the Spirit of God, which is stronger than steel or darkness.

Also, spider webs can be destroyed with one pass of the hand. But no matter how many we get rid of, spiders keep rebuilding them. The world has made innumerable attempts to get rid of the church, beginning with the Romans and continuing on through Communist persecutions. But the church is pesky and persistent; it keeps coming back. And it will keep coming back again and again until Jesus himself comes back again.

Finally, though flimsy and holey, Lydia's spider web made the perfect gift for the newborn child. Our church is a gift too. It's not perfect by any means. But it has a miraculous ability to foil Roman soldiers and protect the future of a king.

So let's take a closer look at the church. In fact, while we're on the subject of creating, let's examine everything it takes to make a congregation from scratch: denominations, ministers, youth ministers, choir leaders, church buildings, educational programs, worship services, ushers, singles, couples, people who sharpen the little pew pencils, and elves who sneak in at night and *unsharpen* the pew pencils.

And most important, let's find out what to do with five tons of green-bean casserole left over from the latest potluck dinner.

Whether we're creating a church or a spider web, there's no better model than the ultimate creative act: the creation of the universe. So in the following seven chapters we'll look at seven key areas of the church and see how closely they parallel the seven days of creation.

Let the spinning begin.

THE FIRST DAY

The Baptists Are Separated from the Episcopalians

And God said, "Let there be light," and there was light. God saw that the light was good, and he separated the light from the darkness. God called the light "day," and the darkness he called "night." And there was evening, and there was morning—the first day.

GENESIS 1:3–5

When God created the universe, he made something out of nothing, which highlights a major difference between God and people. When God makes something out of nothing, it is a positive act that brings planets and stars and comets into being. When people make something out of nothing it usually means they've been spending too much time arguing about the color of the curtains in the fellowship hall.

Over the years, arguments about matters both trivial and non-trivial have led to the creation of countless denominations. Although this has caused a lot of confusion, it's not reason for despair. As Genesis says, God brought order to a chaotic primeval world. So it is safe to say that God can also work wonders through a chaotic hodge-podge of denominations.

What Type of Church Government?

The first consideration when deciding on a denomination is how much bureaucracy you want to create. Basically, there are two kinds of church government to choose from: centralized and independent.

Centralized churches take orders from denominational headquarters situated in distant cities—usually Washington, D.C., or New York. The concrete in those cities grows excellent bureaucracies, just like Iowa soil grows great corn. In fact, red tape is New York's third largest industry, right behind mugging and driving taxis with amplified horns and no brakes.

The problem with a centralized church government is that contacting the denominational office is about as complicated as contacting a U.S. government office. If the Roman jailer in Acts 16 had tried to call a denominational office, he might have encountered something like this:

Switchboard Operator at Denominational Headquarters: Denominational Headquarters. How may I help you?

Jailer: I would like to know what I must do to be saved.

Switchboard Operator: Hold, please. (*Twenty minutes later.*) Hello, what can I do for you?

Jailer: I've been on hold for about twenty minutes and—!

Switchboard Operator: Only twenty minutes? I'm sorry. Let me put you on hold again. (*Ten minutes later.*) Okay, what can I do for you?

Jailer: I would like to know what I must do to be saved.

Switchboard Operator: Oh, I'm sorry. You have the wrong department. You've reached the Center for Souls Looking for Answers to Questions Asked by Smart-Aleck Kids in Sunday School—CSLAQASAKSS. What you want is the Division of People Who Are Looking for a Godly Time—DPWALFGT. I'll transfer the call.

Jailer: But—

DPWALFGT Recording: Hello, you have reached the DPWALFGT. If you have a touch-tone phone and wish to talk to someone about theological issues, press one. If you wish to talk to someone about what to do with green-bean casseroles left over from church potlucks, press two. If you wish to confess your sins, press three. If you wish to debate whether Protestant churches should get into Bingo, press four. If you want to know what you must do to be saved, press five. If you . . .

The Roman jailer presses five.

DPWALFGT Recording: Hello, you have reached the Division of Lost Souls. If you have a touch-tone phone and wish to talk to someone about whether you're once saved, always saved, press one. If you wish to talk to someone about whether hell is really hot or whether it's just the humidity, press two. If you wish to talk . . .

After reading this scenario, you may think centralized churches are inferior to independent churches. But that's not necessarily true. Independent churches have their problems too because usually they are accountable to no one. As a result, they often come up with really off-the-wall beliefs. This is especially true when the church is comprised mainly of *new* Christians.

For example, there's been intense controversy over a church of newly converted bicycle thieves who keep snipping prayer chains. There is also an unusual church on Broadway made up entirely of newly converted actors who believe the world will end when God shouts, "Five minutes everybody!"

Probably the strangest belief has arisen in a church of newly converted National Park rangers who maintain that every person's spirit is omnipresent (i.e., in all places at all times). This belief became evident when one of the rangers posted a new hiking map with an arrow indicating, "You are here," as well as arrows indicating, "You are also here, here, here, here, here, here, here, here, and here."

Choosing a Personality

Another major task to accomplish before selecting a denomination is to decide what kind of personality your church should have. Should it be a freewheeling church where people raise hands and shout "Amen"? Should it be a quiet, reserved congregation? Or should you try the trickiest route of all—make it a mixture of freewheeling and reserved?

For a good model of how to do the latter, I refer to the First Church of Especially Swell People, Reformed—one of America's largest nonexistent churches. Christians there have been conducting Strategic Arms Reduction Talks (START) ever since their pastor decided to unite those who prefer a more formal service and those who have become part of the charismatic movement.

The most controversial part of the START treaty has been the arms limitation clause. Proponents of a more formal service stipulated that only two arms could be raised at any time during the service, and a total of only twenty arms during an entire service.

Both sides appeared unified on this compromise until the charismatics took advantage of a loophole and started sticking their feet into the air.

Work will soon begin on Feet and Arms Reduction Talks.

What About Rituals?

The next thing to decide is whether to be a plain, straightforward type of church or to be liturgical—with rituals, vestments, and all. One warning here: The people who get annoyed with formality may go into orbit when you introduce liturgy. Usually, however, this is only because they don't understand its value. If you explain the practicality of such things as vestments—they conceal sweat stains when preachers raise their arms on hot days—most people will eventually come to appreciate the benefits of symbols and rituals.

Choosing a Denomination

Once you have decided on a personality for your church, it's time to pick a denomination to match. Don't limit yourself to the major denominations like Baptist, Lutheran, Methodist, Presbyterian, Catholic, etc. Some of the less popular ones are the most intriguing.

One example is the Amish. They believe that modern technology is harmful to spiritual health. If you have ever tried to hook up a new VCR, you know this is true because the temptation to cuss increases twenty-fold. The temptation increases thirty-fold if the product is imported and the directions were translated by someone who studied English in his spare time after working a twenty-hour day. Such directions are easily recognizable because they read like this: "You shall putting together the video cassette recorder in such a way that for this you will connect cords that are to be chosen for between audio input and, if picture is desirable quantity, the video input."

IN OTHER WORDS

Things that All Denominations Have in Common

While all denominations have their differences, they also have their similarities. In fact, no matter which denomination you choose, there are certain things you can't avoid. They are common to all churches. To satisfy my own curiosity, I've been compiling a list. Study it closely so you won't be surprised when these things happen in your church.

Altar-Callbacks. The feeling that you should answer an altar call for the fifteenth time, just to make sure you've really committed your life to Jesus.

Bapcubes. Water molecules, found only in baptismals, that stay at a constant temperature just above freezing. If you fill a baptismal with scalding hot water, these molecules change the water's temperature to Arctic levels in approximately two seconds.

Bluffering. A technique performed during the offering in which you pretend to search your pockets for money (even though you don't intend to put any money in the plate). This keeps you from looking like a total cheapskate when you pass the offering plate without putting anything into it.

Bozone. The part of a church service when nobody knows what's supposed to happen next and everyone is waiting for somebody to do something.

Church Glands

Church Glands. Special glands in your palms that create sweat whenever you're asked to join hands with other people during a song or prayer.

Fumblerumble. The static-like rumbling sound that occurs when a preacher is clipping a microphone to his tie.

Genderbenders. The name given to accidents in which a man mistakenly starts singing during the women's part of the hymn, or vice versa.

Hushlunging. A skill mastered by churchgoers who are tone deaf in which they sing so softly that people beside them can't hear them.

Fumblerumble

Hymnpickled. The inability to locate the right song in the hymnal until the congregation is into the last verse. This is accompanied by the tendency to peer at the hymnal of the person next to you.

Leavepeeve. The fear that if you leave to go to the bathroom during the sermon people will think you are angry about something the preacher said.

Legfenders. The parts of your leg that bump against the leg of a person who is trying to squeeze past you in the pew.

Miracle. A word used by choir members who find a choir robe that fits.

Miracle

Oldidote. Any anecdote that has been used in a sermon more than twenty times during a single year.

Pew Rubble. Pieces of paper and unclaimed bulletins that are left in pews after a service is over.

Riptide. The sound of checks being ripped from checkbooks during the quietest, most reverent part of a church service.

Sermends. Parts of a sermon that sound like the conclusion but end up being a transition to a whole new section. They are most common during sermons in which a pastor says "In closing" more than a dozen times.

Whaaaa! Pollen

Skiptunes. The verses of a hymn that the songleader always leaves out, usually the second and third.

Solonut. A person who doesn't realize that he or she is clapping on a different beat of the song than everyone else.

Whaaaa! Pollen. Particles given off by a baby crying in church, causing all other babies to start crying.

Woopsoid. A person who accidentally starts the next verse of a song three seconds before the rest of the congregation.

ODD-SERVATIONS

*An Inside Look at the First Church of Especially Swell People, Reformed**

Practical jokes are routine in the friendly rivalry between the First Church of Especially Swell People, Reformed, and the Lutheran church down the street. In this photo, the Lutheran pastor tells members of our church why his denomination believes in baptism by sprinkling.

* Photos courtesy of Bud Kelso, First Church photographer.

Teenagers at a nearby non-instrumentalist church rejoiced when their denomination agreed to make an exception to its ban on musical instruments. Teens *could* play instruments during church, as long as they only performed "air guitar" or "air organ."

Inter-denominational unity is at an all-time high during the Christian Olympics. Here, First Church's head usher, Bob Holliman, comes away with a bronze medal in the offering dish toss. He not only tossed the dish 176 feet, but he collected $567 in the process.

Meanwhile, a team of Trappist monks took the gold in the 400-meter contemplative relay, while the Quaker team swept all medals in pacifist boxing—a contest to see which boxer can turn the other cheek the most times.

The most popular event at the Olympics is the church bus marathon, a race in which churches compete to see which bus can travel the farthest before breaking down. The Baptists hold the record at 452 feet.

For a while, it looked as if shy people in churches nationwide were going to start their own denomination, complete with shy hymns, such as: "When the Saints Go Marching In, I Want to Remain Inconspicuous" and "It's a Silent Night, Holy Night When Nobody Expects Me to Initiate Conversations."

As it turned out, shy people decided *not* to split off and create their own denomination, primarily because churches like ours formed vibrant ministries to shy people. In the picture above, a special Bible study for shy people is underway, although it is believed that nobody has yet said a word in the last two years. "We clear our throats a lot," says the shy Bible study leader, who was too embarrassed to reveal his name. The group stands by its motto: "We show up, don't we?"

REAL LIFE

Gnats, Camels, Lions, and Other Church Animals

It was a bad day for the Pharisees. They approached Jesus, probably to try to trick him into saying something blasphemous, as they had tried so many times before, but they ended up with egg on their own faces.

Whatever their intentions, they evidently didn't get to carry them out. Jesus beat them to the punch, laying into them with what has become known as "the seven woes." Jesus revealed, one after another, all of the flaws and foibles of the Pharisees. And in public, of all places. How embarrassing.

For instance, in Matthew 23:23–24, Jesus says, "Woe to you, teachers of the law and Pharisees, you hypocrites! You give a tenth of your spices—mint, dill, and cummin. But you have neglected the more important matters of the law—justice, mercy, and faithfulness. You should have practiced the latter, without neglecting the former. You blind guides! You strain out a gnat but swallow a camel."

When you read those words, how do you picture Jesus?

Chances are, you probably imagine him looking angry. Why? As Elton Trueblood says in his book *The Humor of Christ,* how do we know that Jesus wasn't smiling? After all, he had just conjured up a crazy image.

Strict Pharisees often strained their drinking water through a cloth to make sure they did not swallow a gnat, the smallest of unclean animals. But while they were busy straining gnats out of their water, they gulped down an entire camel—the *largest* of unclean animals.

Here's how the English scholar T. R. Glover describes it: "The long hairy neck slid down the throat of the Pharisee—all that amplitude of loose-hung anatomy—the hump—two humps—both of them slid down—and he never noticed—and the legs—all of them—with the whole outfit of knees and big padded feet. The Pharisee swallowed a camel and never noticed it."

The image would make a great Looney Tunes cartoon.

According to Trueblood, the humor here is not vicious. Jesus uses it to attack the legalism of the Pharisees, but he's not ridiculing an individual Pharisee.

Jesus doesn't stop with one attack. He moves to an equally comical picture in Matthew 23:25–26. "Woe to you, teachers of the law and Pharisees, you hypocrites!" he tells them. "You clean the outside of the cup and dish, but inside they are full of greed and self-indulgence. Blind Pharisee! First clean the inside of the cup and dish, and then the outside also will be clean."

Was Jesus smiling when he spoke those words? Surely somebody in the crowd must have been smiling. It was a wild picture. Imagine a man at his kitchen sink, arms buried in soap suds, scrubbing frantically on the *outside* of his treasured cup. When he finally gets the outside as polished as marble, the guy fills it with sparkling clean water and gulps it down, not even noticing that the cup is filled with dead spiders, dust balls, dirt, and a few flies.

It seems strange that we almost never imagine Jesus smiling or laughing when he says the things he does. We either picture him angry or mystical-looking.

Franco Zeffirelli's movie *Jesus of Nazareth* is a great show in many ways, but it portrays Jesus about as solemn as they come. He hardly ever cracked a smile. And I'm pretty sure he never blinked. I think he spent the entire movie staring.

This kind of image distorts Christ's full character. Jesus was fully human and fully God, so he *must* have blinked or he would have gone blind. Likewise, a fully human Jesus must have laughed. Laughter is an essential part of being human. Jesus was passionate. In the New Testament, we see him get angry, cry, celebrate, and feel both sadness and apprehension. That's the miracle of the incarnation—God entering a human body and experiencing every human emotion.

That's also the miracle of the church. For two thousand years now, the church has tried to balance a body of people as diverse as the emotions inside each of us. The church crosses an incredible range of cultures, temperaments, and worship styles. The truth of the Gospel stays the same, but the ways we celebrate the truth are as diverse as they come—everything from Eastern Orthodox priests in elaborate garb to Pentecostal healers in rolled-up shirt sleeves.

The balancing act isn't easy. In the same way that many of us feel uncomfortable with the idea of Jesus laughing, some of us feel uncomfortable with churchgoers who express themselves in different ways. We get annoyed when worshipers raise their hands. Or make the sign of the cross. Or wear vestments. Or don't wear vestments. Or genuflect. Or shout "Hallelujah." Or pray quietly.

We like our churches to be uniform because uniformity is comforting in that it confirms our belief that we are right. This preference is natural, but it's not fair.

We have the same problem when the Bible talks about a time in the future when the lion will lie down with the lamb. We assume that the lion will become tame and lamblike, but is that being fair to the lion? How do we know that the lion and lamb won't retain their basic temperaments and still make peace? After all, there's nothing wrong with being a lion.

As G. K. Chesterton points out, "The real problem is—Can the lion lie down with the lamb and still retain his royal ferocity? *That* is the problem the church attempted; *that* is the miracle she achieved."

God is the master of wild things and tame things, extroverts and introverts, Pentecostals and non-Pentecostals. But that shouldn't surprise us. God himself is both the Lion of Judah and the Lamb of God.

He can be meek. He can roar.

REAL LIFE

Giving Away Church Members

Jesus is not a polygamist, says Juan Carlos Ortiz, an Argentinean evangelist. Jesus has one bride. One church.

Most of us recognize that there really exists only one Christian church, despite our tendency to give it a myriad of denominational labels. But do we really *behave* as if there is one church?

I get a kick out of Juan Carlos Ortiz because his church in Argentina actually practiced what it preached about the oneness of the church. Here are just a few examples, gleaned from *The Door Interviews* and Ortiz's book *Disciple*.

* * *

Not far from Ortiz's Pentecostal church in Argentina, there was an Anglican church where the minister spoke very little Spanish. The Anglican church had only about seven English-speaking members left, while Ortiz's church had one thousand. Ortiz said that if their church believed in unity, some of their members would go across town and announce to the Anglican minister, "We're here to become members of your church."

Fifty members did just that. They became full members of the Anglican church, accepting new traditions such as bishops, processionals, garments, and candles.

* * *

When Ortiz tried to form bonds with other pastors in his community, he didn't begin the usual way. With meetings.

"Pastors are tired of meetings," Ortiz says.

Instead, he began by forming a relationship with two or three other pastors. They did things together. Backpacking. Meeting each other's families. Going out for ice cream.

"If I invite a Baptist minister to my meetings, he won't come because he is anti-charismatic and I am charismatic," he adds. "But if I invite him over for ice cream, he is not anti-ice cream, so he would come . . . After you are friends, the barriers can be ignored."

A Catholic priest invited Ortiz to preach in Montevideo, Uruguay, and the event drew thousands of converts to Christ. Most of the converts came from a Catholic background, but Ortiz decided that his job wasn't to change them into Protestants.

Instead, Ortiz formed a Catholic branch of their evangelical Protestant church—a branch made up of about two hundred people. As time went by, a Catholic priest came to their fellowship and concluded that he hadn't really been committed to Jesus.

"We have been waiting for you," Ortiz told the priest. "We have two hundred believers that belong to you."

We have a long tradition of grouping ourselves by brand names, such as Methodist, Presbyterian, Catholic, Nazarene, and First Church of Especially Swell People, Reformed. But that's not the way the Holy Spirit groups people, Ortiz says. The Spirit's grouping is much more clear, clean, and simple. Just two categories: Those who love one another and those who don't.

ORIGINS

Methodists. The name "Methodist" was originally a name of scorn. When John Wesley organized a group of Oxford University students, they followed a certain program, or "method," of study and worship. Their methods attracted ridicule from other students, who started calling them "Methodists." One consolation is that the name beat some of their other nicknames—"Bible Bigots" and "Bible Moths," for instance.

Lutherans. Here's another name rooted in ridicule. Catholics came up with the name "Lutherans" to describe Martin Luther's followers. But Luther didn't like the name. He preferred that his followers be called "Evangelicals."

Presbyterians. The name "Presbyterian" is based on the Greek word *presbuteros*, which means "elder."

Anglicans. Want to irritate an Anglican? Tell him that his church was started just so a king could squirm out of a marriage. There's some truth in it. When the pope wouldn't annul Henry VIII's marriage to Catherine of Aragon, the king declared himself head of a new church—the Church of England, the Anglican Church. Then he gave himself an annulment.

The situation was more complicated than that, however. The English had been battling with the pope for over one hundred years and a break with Rome probably would have come anyway.

Quakers. A fellow known as Justice Bennet was given credit for coming up with the name "Quaker" upon hearing the group's founder, George Fox, bid his people to "quake and tremble at the word of the Lord."

Eastern Orthodox. When people divide the church into Protestants and Catholics, they are forgetting someone—the Eastern Orthodox Church, which is most prevalent in Eastern Europe and the Eastern Mediterranean.

Originally, the Christian church was one body, governed by five patriarchs in five cities. There was one patriarch in the West—the pope—and four patriarchs in the East. But the East and the West kept having theological and political squabbles. And all the cultural differences didn't help the situation.

This eventually led to the "Great Schism" in 1054, which split the church in half. The pope excommunicated one of the patriarchs from the eastern church. In turn, the patriarch excommunicated the pope.

First Church of Especially Swell People, Reformed. This denomination consists of one fictional church in a city that wishes to remain anonymous to protect its reputation. The name was chosen in 1873 after a close eighty-eight to eighty-five vote. This is significant because only forty people attended the meeting where the vote took place.

THE SECOND DAY

Let There Be Ministers

And God said, "Let there be an expanse between the waters to separate water from water." So God made the expanse and separated the water under the expanse from the water above it. And it was so. God called the expanse "sky." And there was evening, and there was morning—the second day.

GENESIS 1:6–8

God created the sky on the second day, so it makes sense that the second day in the creation of a church should deal with ministers. The sky and pastors have a lot in common.

Churchgoers like to look up to their pastors, just as they enjoy gazing up at the sky. In fact, this may explain why some churches construct their pulpits so far off the ground that it takes a two-day expedition with Sherpa guides for people to reach the top.

However, churchgoers put their ministers in a bind. They want them to be lofty so they can look up to them, but they also want them to be down-to-earth so they can relate to them.

Seminaries do a lot to prepare ministers for the lofty part of the job because they encourage would-be ministers to grapple with tough, high-minded questions like, "Is it possible to lose your salvation or is it only possible to misplace it?"

But seminaries need to work more on the down-to-earth part. If seminaries want to provide valuable on-the-job experience, they should offer a class that meets at one-thirty in the morning. Students would need to bring paper, a pencil, pajamas, and a toothbrush. Then they would be required to fall asleep at their desks, only to be awakened at three o'clock by a prominent member of the church calling to find out if anyone found her casserole dish, which she left in the church kitchen after the potluck two weeks ago.

This is what being a minister is really all about.

How to "Call" a Minister

When you're ready to select a minister, the procedure usually goes like this: Get a committee together, talk about a bunch of candidates, and then "cal!" one of them.

When appointing the pastoral selection committee, make sure you select especially perceptive people because you cannot allow even the smallest comments to go unnoticed. For instance, selection committee members should be concerned if they hear one of the applicants say, "God has really convicted me. Incidentally, so has the state of Florida."

After selecting the selection committee and interviewing the candidates, you are ready for the actual call. To illustrate how to proceed in this, I refer you to my mother. She had two "call" strategies: the soft approach and the tough approach. With the soft approach, she opened the back door and calmly called, "Doug! Come on in for dinner now!" With the tough approach, she opened the back door and yelled, "Douglas *Gerard* Peterson!! Come in this instant!" And I would come running home as quickly as humanly possible because the last thing I wanted was to have my mom broadcasting to the entire neighborhood that my middle name was Gerard.

Come to think of it, getting kids to come in the house promptly may be the primary reason parents give their children middle names. Why else would so many kids have such weird middle names as Mordecai, Percival, or Goober?

What I'm trying to say through all of this is that if a church wants to get a quick response when they "call" a minister, they should use my mom's tough approach. The entire committee should shuffle to the back door, open the screen, and yell, "Rev. Robert *Boregarde* Thompkins! Come in the church this minute!!"

I guarantee that Rev. Robert Boregarde Thompkins will be at your church door faster than you could say Boregarde. Be aware, however, that using a person's middle name in public could be grounds for a lawsuit.

One last point about calling a minister. Don't say, "Here minister, minister. Here minister, minister (whistle, whistle, whistle). That's a good minister."

I say this because treating ministers like dogs is one of the greatest problems in churches today. In his book *All Preachers Great and Small*, Rev. John Herriot mentions one church that has trained its pastor to fetch, roll over, heel, and sit on hundreds of senseless committees.

"We're fortunate to have a pure-bred pastor who is a real good pointer," says Sylvia Wilson, a member of this church, which prefers to remain anonymous. "Whenever the deacons take him soul-winning, he runs around pointing at sinners and barking his head off.

"It's just a shame that our last pastor didn't work out," she adds. "We had to have him put to sleep, which is ironic since he was the one who usually put *us* to sleep."

Speaking of Sleep

Pastors do need at least a few hours of sleep every night. After all, they are human. People generally forget this, though. In fact, congregations that treat their pastor like a dog usually expect him to perform like an entire Ringling Brothers Barnum & Bailey Circus. They expect him to be a great administrator, great preacher, great teacher, great counselor, great parent, great prayer warrior—and on and on.

Just last week I got to feeling so sorry for my minister that I called him up at a time when I was pretty sure he'd be home—three in the morning—and I said, "Ron, you're doing a great job. I just thought you needed to know."

"Huh . . . wha . . . blhbm?" Ron said sleepily, but I could tell that he was truly touched by my appreciation.

The Mediator

One of the most important qualities of a minister is counseling skills. A pastor must be able to help people resolve differences. A minister is a mediator, and the function of a mediator is to take all of the punches.

Ask anyone who has ever watched a hockey game. When two play-ers get into a fight, the referee (the only guy *without* protective gear) gets into the middle and tries to break it up. In the process, he usually gets hit with all of the punches. Meanwhile, the two players skate away smiling about how they were able to get revenge on the referee for his earlier calls.

So the next time you see your minister, say something nice. Smile. Then offer to buy him some protective hockey gear.

SERMONS FOR THE RICH AND FAMOUS

No chapter about pastors is complete without a word about sermons. Sermons are the focal point of just about every church service, and some churches believe sermons are so important that they have two— one for adults and one for kids. And usually the one for kids is better. So why not make every sermon a children's sermon? After all, Jesus said that to enter the kingdom of heaven we should be like little children.

But you may wonder why we should model ourselves after creatures who have the ability to ask, "Can I have more ice cream?" seven thousand times in one thirty-minute period.

I'll tell you why. Children are the only people humble enough to get in front of an entire congregation, sit on the floor, and listen to a children's sermon every week. I have never seen one child (a young one at least) say he or she is too dignified to sit cross-legged on the floor in front of a teacher.

To help adults learn to be childlike, I propose that each week the pastor aim a children's sermon at a group of adults in need of humility. We *all* need our pride popped on a regular basis, so one week the children's sermon would be aimed at doctors, the next week at lawyers, and the next week at smart-aleck writers of books like this.

Wouldn't it be great to see about a dozen lawyers, three-piece suits and all, shuffle out of their pews, acting shy and confused, while their spouses say encouraging things like, "Go on up front and sit down. Don't be shy! You appear in front of people in court every week. You can do it." Then all of the lawyers would get down on the floor at the feet of their teacher who is sitting on a stool and talking to them with puppets.

I guarantee this will make them considerably more humble. Of course, it will also probably make them considerably more interested in attending another church, but every new idea has a few bugs in it.

For those churches bold enough to try this remarkable new idea, I have provided a sample sermon. This one is to be used with the wealthiest members of the church, or anyone else facing the temptations of mammon. The story is called "Noah's Wallet." So if you kids will just settle down, I'll begin.

Noah's Wallet

Gerald G. Noah thought it was strange that the angel visiting him looked like Karl Malden—the guy who does TV commercials about traveler's checks. But the angel's message was even more startling.

"Mr. Noah," said this angel wearing a trench coat. "The Lord would like to warn you that the world is going to experience an economic catastrophe like none that has been seen before."

Gulp. "And what would the Lord like of me?" Gerald G. Noah said, trembling.

"Be as wise as Solomon," the angel said. "The catastrophe approaches." Then he vanished into thin air (which is a lot trickier than vanishing into fat air).

Gerald G. Noah pondered the unusual visitation for the rest of the day and into the night. By morning he had decided what he would do.

"Wife," he said, "gather together our sons. We're going to build a wallet!"

And so Gerald G. Noah began to build a huge wallet, three hundred cubits long by fifty cubits wide by thirty cubits high. This, he said, would protect them during the financial collapse. By stuffing the wallet with money, they would survive the disaster.

So Gerald G. Noah's sons sewed together the colossal seams, while he went across the land, gathering money, two hundred by two hundred. He gathered two hundred of every type of money, and then he jammed all of it into the wallet. American dollars. English pounds. German marks. Japanese yen. Italian lira. Mexican pesos.

But that was not all. Gerald G. Noah also collected two of every kind of credit card on the face of the earth. He encased them in sleeves of clear plastic and slipped them into the wallet.

He even purchased two giant-sized pictures of perfect strangers, male and female, like those that come with every new wallet. Then, with the addition of a few more forms of money, the wallet was complete. Gerald G. Noah had built his wallet of protection.

Mrs. Noah suggested that a giant purse would provide more room than an oversized wallet, but Gerald G. Noah said he didn't have the time or energy to fill a purse with two of every type of cosmetic on the face of the earth. So a wallet it was.

Gerald G. Noah was sixty-five years old when the economic disaster struck. Then Mr. Noah and his sons and his wife and his sons' wives went into the wallet. With one last look at the world, they pulled shut the large zipper they had constructed to keep others out.

Wall Street collapsed for forty days and forty nights, and people lost everything they ever owned. Waves of depression crashed upon the earth, drowning people in financial ruin, debt, misery, and poverty.

The debts and disaster increased and bore upon the wallet. Banks collapsed. Corporations went bankrupt. Farms were auctioned. But Gerald G. Noah? He and his family were secure, snug in their money-packed wallet.

Finally, the wave of doom began to diminish, slowing down to a trickle, and the huge debts began to recede on the face of the earth.

Now Gerald G. Noah, sensing this change in the economic climate, decided to send out a raven to see if all was safe. The raven flew to and fro across the earth; but the bird couldn't land a good job anywhere, so he returned to the wallet empty-beaked. That is how Gerald G. Noah knew it was still unsafe to leave the wallet.

Next, Gerald G. Noah sent out a dove. After two such attempts, the dove returned with a paycheck in its beak, a sign that the economy had improved.

So Gerald G. Noah and his family opened their wallet to the light of day and stepped out upon the land. And lo, the angel was waiting for them there, tapping his right foot and looking disgusted.

"Gerald G. Noah," the angel said. "The Lord told you to deal with this disaster by imitating the *wisdom* of Solomon, not the *greed* of Solomon."

"But I just wanted to protect myself. I had to make sure I was financially secure. Don't you see? Like the Noah of old, I had to—"

"The Noah of old was asked to protect and preserve the entire creation, and that he did," the angel said forcefully. "But you protected nobody but yourself. The Lord wanted you to use your vast resources to help people who were destroyed by the economic disaster. He didn't ask you to hoard it all!"

But alas, Gerald G. Noah was not listening to the angel. He was looking at a rainbow that arched across the cloudless sky.

"Look!" he said, pointing at the rainbow. "The Lord has sent a sign to show me that hoarding my money *was* the right thing to do."

Remembering the legend that says a pot of gold sits at the end of every rainbow, Gerald G. Noah sprinted off in pursuit of the loot. He was sure the Lord was going to reward him big time.

But his vision was an illusion. There was no pot of gold at the end of the rainbow. And when he returned home, he learned that his huge wallet had been stolen—lifted by a team of one hundred pickpockets.

"I'm destroyed!" Gerald G. Noah sobbed. "I have nothing! Nothing at all! No pesos. No dollars. No rubles. No—"

"Do you have treasures stored in heaven?" someone said.

Gerald G. Noah looked up and saw that it was the angel who had spoken, the angel in a trench coat.

"The Bible says to store up your treasures in heaven, not on earth," the angel said. "Do you have any treasures in heaven?"

Gerald G. Noah could only shake his head "no" and sob some more.

And lo, as a crowd began to form around the poor man, the angel turned to them and said, "Treasures in heaven. Don't leave home without them."

Sponsor a Pastor

Help relieve suffering through 'Pastor-Compassion, International'

You Can Make a Difference

When confronted with the world's problems, many people feel helpless. But now, you *can* help. Pastor-Compassion, International enables you to have an impact in the life of one special person—a minister. Pastors spend so much time in meetings that most suffer severe bouts of boredom and fatigue. Now you can relieve their suffering by donating a little bit of your time every month. Only a couple of hours will do it.

So how does Pastor-Compassion, International work?

When you sponsor a pastor, you commit yourself to attending just one of his meetings every month. Your support can free him to do things he never has time to do—things like go on vacation or visit the rest room.

How Do I Know if I'm Really Helping?

Our program is a very personal one. Every month, your pastor will send you a photograph of himself spending time with his family or maybe even a picture of himself getting sleep for a change. That way, you know that your contribution is making a difference.

Don't put it off! Join the growing number of caring people who have discovered the special joy of sponsoring a needy pastor.

Membership Form

Yes, I would like to sponsor a pastor who needs a break today. I prefer a

_____ Methodist	_____ Baptist	_____ Catholic
_____ Assembly of God	_____ Church of Especially Swell People, Reformed	

Name _____

Address _____

City _____ State _____ Zip _____

Type of coffee I prefer:

_____ Black	_____ Cream and Sugar	_____ Sugar Only
_____ Cream Only	_____ Decaffeinated	_____ Enough caffeine to stun a bull

Type of meetings I prefer:

_____ Business Meetings	_____ Meetings where the last two hours are spent repeating what people said during the first two hours.	_____ Meetings where the chairperson doesn't really act in charge and kinda lets things drag on and on with long, uncomfortable silences.
_____ Social Meetings	_____ Meetings where the chairperson asks, "Does anyone have anything else to say?" and you sit there praying, "Please, please, don't anybody say anything else so we can go home," and just before the chairperson is about to close the meeting someone brings up another topic that takes another forty-five minutes to discuss.	

ODD-SERVATIONS

An Inside Look at the First Church of Especially Swell People, Reformed*

Pastor Bobo's children will do anything to be with their father, who spends most of his time at meetings. Last week, for instance, Joshua and Esther disguised themselves as Episcopal ministers so they could talk with their father at a monthly meeting among community ministers. Pastor Bobo didn't even catch on to their disguises until the ministers shared prayer concerns. That's when Joshua asked the ministers to pray that he could learn how to create artificial burps.

* Photos courtesy of Bud Kelso, First Church photographer.

Last year it became obvious that our ministers were afraid of giving challenging sermons (they feared losing their jobs). So they decided to only preach when their faces are hidden by a blue dot—the kind of dot you see on the Cable News Network. As a result, nobody knows which of our four pastors is giving the challenging sermon.

Pastor Bobo is pleased with the new "altar call waiting" system, in which he uses six phones and handles up to a dozen altar calls at the same time. New converts don't always like being put on hold, but at least it's better than the previous system in which phones were placed in every pew hymnal rack and Pastor Bobo spent half of the service calling people and asking for commitments to Christ. He soon learned that many are called, but most leave their phone off the hook.

This is a must-have accessory for every pastor—a Salvation Army Knife. Developed by First Church's Russell Milhouse, the Salvation Army Knife includes a pocket Bible, miniature cherry pie (for emergency potluck dinners), church bell, knife, offering plate, and pot of coffee (for long, long, long meetings).

REAL LIFE

Calling All Fools

The church needs more fools in the ministry.

In fact, all seminaries should require students to take a course on the art of foolishness. One of their prime subjects would be a youth who lived in the thirteenth century. Consider his record.

✳ ✳ ✳

This youth had his head filled with dreams of knighthood. So he convinced his father to spend an armload of money on the finest suit of armor you could buy. Then the young man marched off to battle in a distant land.

The first night on the road, the youth fell into a feverish sleep and thought he heard a voice telling him to go back home. The next day, he returned home without a single chink on his armor. A blemish-free breastplate was the mark of a coward.

"What happened?" exclaimed his father, who was not too happy to see an expensive piece of equipment go to waste. The armor cost almost as much as a farm.

"A voice told me to come back home," said his son.

The father rolled his eyes.

✳ ✳ ✳

Instead of following some great and glorious goal, the youth returned to his old life—drinking and carousing with friends. Then one night, in the middle of a glutton's feast, he fell in love.

He fell in love with God.

And the youth began giving money to every beggar he encountered, for he had been dubbed a knight of God.

Riding through the afternoon countryside, this knight of God encountered something more horrifying than all the armies of Islam. He saw a leper, with sores blazing across his partially paralyzed face. And the smell! It was beyond belief. The knight of God wanted to run or throw up or do both. But he knew what the Lord wanted him to do.

The knight jumped down from his horse, and the poor leper jumped back in alarm, thinking he was about to be attacked. But to the leper's surprise, the knight of God didn't club him over the head. The knight did a most incredible thing. He took the leper by the shoulders and planted a holy kiss on those shredded lips.

As he walked away from the baffled leper and returned to his horse, the knight began to sing.

When the knight of God came across a church that was falling apart, he heard a voice say, "Repair my house." His conclusion: God was telling him to rebuild the crumbling church.

To do the job, he needed to raise money. Fast. So he went to his father's store, where rich fabrics were stored, took a few expensive samples, went out, and sold them.

The furious father dragged his wacky son before a public court and said he wanted his son to renounce all claims to his inheritance.

Standing before a crowd of gapers in a public square, the youth was quite happy to renounce his claim to the inheritance. In fact, he renounced his claim to everything. Including his clothes. The goofball took off his clothes, threw them at his father's feet, dropped the bag of gold on top of the heap, and began to march off into the woods like a knight in naked armor.

"I shall go naked to meet the Lord," he declared.

The father felt a mixture of shame and fury. Do you blame him?

After an observer gave his cloak to the naked youth, the knight of God marched deep into the forest singing. Along the way, he encountered a group of thieves.

"I am the herald of the Great King!" the youth declared when asked to identify himself. But the thugs just laughed, stole his cloak, and threw him into a snowbank. After waiting for the thieves to walk away, the youth got to his feet, brushed off the snow, and began to sing once again.

Looking at the bare facts of his life, you might conclude that this guy had recently been kicked in the head by a horse. But as his life unfolded, hundreds and then millions of people became convinced that Francis of Assisi was more than just a fool. He was God's fool. And that's the greatest kind of fool.

Whenever I have a sneaking suspicion that God wants me to do something or say something, the first question that clicks through my brain is, "Will it make me look foolish?" And if I suspect that it will, I usually squelch the urge.

I need to be more of a fool. We all need more foolishness in our lives. The world is desperate for fools. The church needs to set up a Fool Recruitment Center. It needs to organize support groups for fools.

But most of all, it needs fools in leadership.

By fools, I don't mean imbeciles; I mean people who are willing to follow God's leading, even if it makes them look ridiculous. I mean people who are willing to put passion for Jesus ahead of passion for pleasing others.

It's this passion that enables God's fools to go barreling head-first through barriers of inhibition. And it's this passion that enabled Francis to make holiness look like fun.

That's what I call leadership.

Who but Francis of Assisi would think of going before the Islamic sultan, whose armies were battling the Christians, while butchery was taking place on both sides? What a bizarre scene it must have been, this little crust of a man, standing in the sultan's tent and telling him about Jesus.

According to a story related in Julien Green's book *God's Fool,* the sultan had his men lay down a carpet decorated with crosses, and then he commanded Francis to trample on the crosses. With a mischievous glimmer in his eyes, Francis gladly danced on top of them. Then he announced that he had just stepped all over the crosses of the thief who denied Jesus on Calvary.

The sultan scratched his head. "This is one strange guy, but I like him," he must have thought, because he let Francis leave with all of his body parts intact.

One chronicler claimed that when Francis and his dirt-covered followers first appeared before the pope, the pontiff scoffed at them. He mocked Francis by telling him, "Brother, go herd pigs. I should compare you to them rather than to men. Roll in the dunghill with them . . . and be their preacher."

Sure enough, Francis went out of the pope's mighty presence, found the nearest herd of pigs, and rolled around in the mud with them. Then he went back to the pope, who was stunned by this unexpected example of obedience. Then and there, the humbled pope conferred the office of preaching on poor Francis.

If this story isn't true, it should be.

REAL LIFE

Fool Number Two

If Francis of Assisi wasn't foolish enough, meet Don Bosco. This priest wanted to start a new religious order. He wanted to send missionaries all across the world to set up houses for an outreach to boys.

But the church bureaucrats thought he was crazy. Literally.

One church leader, a monsignor, went as far as to make plans to send Don Bosco to an insane asylum, says Fulton F. Sheen in *The Electronic Christian*. The monsignor called for a cab and then motioned for Bosco to get in, not telling him the destination of the carriage. But Bosco knew what the church leader was up to, so he politely said that he wouldn't think of getting into the carriage before the monsignor.

When the monsignor was inside the carriage, Bosco slammed the door shut. He told the driver (a friend of his) to drive to the asylum as quickly as possible because the monsignor was seriously disturbed in the mind.

The monsignor started screaming and shouting at the driver to stop. This behavior only convinced the driver that he did indeed have a crazy person in his carriage, and he rushed the monsignor to the asylum. (The monsignor was eventually able to get his release from the institution's chaplain.)

Like all good leaders, Don Bosco had a vision. In his mind, he could see those missionary houses for boys. But unfortunately, when people see things others can't see, we automatically label them as crazy. Some people who see things *are* crazy, of course. But many are visionaries. They see what we can't see. They hear what we can't hear.

There's an old Jewish story about a deaf man who got lost in the woods. When he finally stumbled across a house, he rushed to the window and peeked inside. What he saw was a room filled with crazy people. Lunatics. They were wildly throwing their bodies all over the place, and they appeared to be laughing, shouting, leaping, and whooping.

Thankful that he had looked into the window before knocking at the door, the deaf man scurried back into the forest and resumed his search for shelter. If only the old man had had ears to hear, he would have known that the people inside were *not* crazy. They were simply dancing and celebrating in a house bulging with music. If only the man could have heard the music . . .

When people peer into the church, they sometimes think we're crazy too. Our job is to make sure they hear the music.

ORIGINS

Clerical Collars. You can thank the Romans for the clerical collar. When Romans spoke in public, they often wore a thin, white scarf around their necks to keep out cold and reduce perspiration stains. In the sixth century, Christian ministers decided to carry on the tradition. The clerical collar was born.

Many ministers today, however, prefer *not* to wear a clerical collar because they believe they can relate better to people if they do not set themselves apart by appearance.

Cassocks and Surplices. The cassock is a black robe often worn by ministers in more liturgical churches. It symbolizes sin. The white surplice goes over the cassock. It symbolizes the forgiveness of Jesus, which covers our sins.

Although the cassock sets a minister apart these days, it was originally chosen because it was the normal attire of Roman men. Ministers were not allowed to wear clothes that made them stand out from other people.

In the sixth century, Romans began switching to more modern clothing, but the ministers kept the tradition of wearing a cassock.

Parson. The minister was sometimes the only educated person in Colonial American towns, and he helped educate others. That's why a minister was sometimes called "the town person." Leave it to those New Englanders, with their accent, to pronounce it as "the town parson." The name stuck.

Reverend. "Reverend" comes from the Latin word *reverendus*, which means "worthy of respect." In seventeenth century England, church-goers coined the term to show their respect to ministers.

Pastor. "Pastor" comes from the Latin word for "shepherd." The connection is clear. Ministers are shepherds of their flocks.

Vicar. "Vicar" has the same origins as the word "vicarious." It means "substitute" or "representative." Vicars represent Christ on earth.

THE **THIRD** DAY

Let There Be Even More Leaders, According to Their Kind

Then God said, "Let the land produce vegetation: seed-bearing plants and trees on the land that bear fruit with seed in it, according to their various kinds." And it was so. The land produced vegetation: plants bearing seed according to their kinds and trees bearing fruit with seed in it according to their kinds. And God saw that it was good. And there was evening, and there was morning—the third day.

GENESIS 1:11–13

On the third day of Creation, plants and trees took form. Therefore, on the third day in the creation of a church it is only natural for various leadership positions to take form and bear fruit with seed in it.

After all, head ministers can't do everything themselves. As the saying goes, "No minister is an island." (However, after attending fifteen years of church socials and eating massive quantities of cake, many of them start to resemble entire continents.)

To provide much-needed assistance in running a congregation, it is a good idea to take the next step in the creation of a church—finding an assistant pastor. A two-person system of leadership works extremely well . . . in most cases.

When the system *doesn't* work, it's often because the senior minister treats his assistant like the most lowly of people—a person who just barely ranks above plant life. Worse yet, some senior ministers treat their assistants like the vice president of the United States.

Like vice-presidents, assistant pastors are often given the most unpleasant tasks. If Mike Wallace calls and says, "I'd like to talk to someone about your church finances for a segment on *60 Minutes*," the odds are pretty good that the call will be given to the assistant pastor. If the church is looking for someone to share the *Four Spiritual Laws* with Saddam Hussein, you can be sure the job will go to the assistant pastor. But worst of all, the assistant pastor is usually the one who must take on the most horrifying, gut-wrenching task of all—finding volunteers.

Finding volunteers is a grueling job because most churchgoers are

already overextended. An assistant pastor needs to be sensitive to this because burn-out can be dangerous, both spiritually and physically. After all, scientists now believe that dinosaurs became extinct because they spent so much time in church meetings that they never had time to mate.

The reason assistant pastors get so little respect is due to what I call "the stupid sidekick syndrome." People have come to expect all two-person teams to include one irritable person and one likable but stupid sidekick.

Think of it . . . Ralph Cramden and Ed Norton. Fred Flintstone and Barney Rubble. Laurel and Hardy. Bert and Ernie. Dick and Tom Smothers.

The good news is that there is a solution to this problem. The assistant pastor hires a third person, someone who gets even less respect.

The youth minister.

The Youth Minister

Youth ministers have the difficult task of dealing with a generation steeped in sex and drugs, a generation that thrives on rebellion, a generation that knows no boundaries. I'm talking, of course, about parents of teenagers.

Youth workers also have to deal with kids who are constantly bombarded with messages telling them that they too are steeped in sex, drugs, and rebellion—not to mention dwindling SAT scores.

But despite the troubles of today's generation, there are many things youth ministers can do to make teens feel important, such as letting them play an active role in church services. If you ask a teen to read a Bible passage in the service, however, make sure it does not include embarrassing words such as "bosom." This could mess up a teenager's entire life.

Ushers

Ushering is an odd position of leadership. I call it "odd" because I have never understood why ushers almost always are men. I mean, it isn't like ushering is a particularly macho job. If it were, John Wayne would've made a movie called *The Leatherneck Ushers of First Baptist Church.*

The actor would have played a tough but tender-hearted commander of a platoon of ushers in a particularly hostile church. In this film, one of his ushers gets injured while trying to get an old-time church member, who is already comfortably situated in his favorite aisle seat in the second row, to move over and make room for a late-comer. The old-timer bops the usher over the head with a pew Bible, and the usher falls to his knees, banging his head on the corner of the pew on his way down and knocking himself unconscious. The old-timer kicks the usher a few times to get him situated properly under the pew and then uses the usher's head as a footstool.

John Wayne sees all this from his lookout position and plans a rescue. He knows he cannot go straight down the aisle. He'd be an easy target for angry deacons who hate it when the service is disrupted. The only way to reach his injured comrade is to go underneath the pews.

"Wa'll, pilgrims," John Wayne says to his fellow ushers crouching at the back of the church. "There comes a time in every man's life when he's gotta do what he's gotta do. And I'm a man, so I'm gonna do what I gotta do if it's the last thing I do."

His comrades warn him that it's too risky, but John Wayne just scoffs, puts a bulletin between his teeth, dives head first under the pew, and begins squirming toward the front of the church on his belly, sliding beneath pointy high heels and dodging sharp pencils thrown by kids in the pews. Finally he reaches his injured buddy and drags him back to safety as organ music thunders all around him and microphone feedback sends shivers up his spine.

Ushers. The few. The proud.

Choir Leaders

On the surface, a choir looks like a peaceful bunch of people who make beautiful sounds. But behind the scenes, a choir can be a soprano-eat-alto environment. This is especially true in churches where you must pass an audition before you can join. The competition can be rough.

A much fairer way for a leader to select choir members is to use this score card. Simply tally up the points and choose those with the highest scores.

QUALITY	SCORE
Tries hard	2
Sings on tune	3
Sings magnificently	4
A possible soloist	5
Brings donuts to rehearsals	12
Donated money for the choir robes	50

In addition to auditions, choir seating arrangements are crucial. You have to find what works for you, but the following arrangement works well for youth choirs.

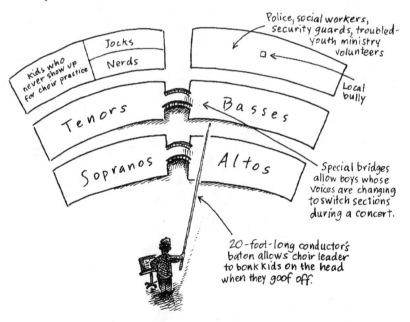

Deacons and Deaconesses

Deacons and deaconesses (or elders, as some churches call them) are usually in charge of checking up on the spiritual life of church members.

To keep in touch with members, it is wise to send people thoughtful notes, preferably specially designed "Christian greeting cards." I have a few examples of greeting cards with a spiritual slant:

"Congratulations on your rapture!"

"Good luck in the afterlife."

"Heard that you sinned . . . Get forgiven soon."

"To Brother on your excommunication."

"Thanks for the challenging sermon, pastor . . . Maybe your next church will like it too. Clean out your desk by Monday."

"When you submit, I feel so close to you."

There can be problems with these cards, however. For instance, it is unkind to send cards to tell people they are not saved. Never send a card that says, "Weather in heaven is good, wish you were going to be there."

SOME POEMS FOR CHURCH LEADERS

The Mind Shepherd

I'm shepherd for some wandering minds
In our Friday fellowship flock.
We try to pray
But our minds, they stray,
Wandering all around the block.

Tom's mind went wandering room to room
And Mary's went out the door.
And Joe's keen mind
I couldn't find.
It had wandered to the store.

Sally's mind was on a trip.
And Bob's was leaving soon.
And Jan's bright mind
Was in a bind.
It's somewhere on the moon.

Shepherding sheep is an easier task
Than keeping minds in line.
So try to be kind.
Keep an eye on your mind.
I think I'm losing mine.

The Committee in My Brain

There's a committee in my brain.
I believe I'm going mad.
They argue all day, fuss all night.
My head hurts real bad.

I wanted a glass of water,
But on that they couldn't agree.
They debated the pros, discussed the cons,
And now I'm still thirs-ty.

The Man Who Ate
from the Offering Plate

A man ate our offering.
I'm not sure why he did it.
A man ate our offering
And wasn't afraid to admit it.

"It's an offering plate," he pointed out.
"Look! Here is my offering fork.
And my other hand holds an offering knife.
So what's the fuss all about?"

A man ate our offering.
I'm not sure why he did it.
A man ate our offering
And wasn't afraid to admit it.

He tucked a napkin beneath his chin,
Then politely asked for salt.
He opened his mouth and scooped up our cash,
Then proceeded to stuff it all in.

A man ate our offering.
I'm not sure why he did it.
A man ate our offering
And wasn't afraid to admit it.

"I could've eaten food. I could've,"
Said the man with the empty plate.
"But if I hadn't eaten the offering,
Our building project would've."

The Schedule

I have a job. I do it well.
I plan the Sunday service.
I keep it moving, keep it busy
'Cause silence makes me nervous.

In my office one day, a bird appeared.
He came without a warning.
He said, "I have a message to give
In church this Sunday morning."

"Hmmmmm," I said, "I just don't know
If we really have the time.
Our schedule is a crowded one.
Adding you might be a crime."

At 10, there is an organ song.
10:10 is John Robb's prayer.
And 10:15 is Tim Lim's time
To stand up and to share.
10:20 we sing some standard hymns.
10:30 is the reading.
10:35 we sing again
While Karen does the leading.
10:40 is the sermon.
The pastor speaks quite well.
11 o'clock we sing once more,
Accompanied by a bell.
11:05—Announcement time.
This lasts forever more.
At 11:15, we shake some hands,
Then hurry for the door.

"You see," I said. "Our schedule's full.
But don't you fear, my dear.

We'll fit you in another day,
Maybe later on this year."

"Gee thanks," said he and then he spoke
So soft I couldn't hear it.
And up he went. That dove flew home.
There goes the Holy Spirit.

The Problem Eater

I don't have any problems.
I'm a leader, and I'm strong.
I'm quite secure. I'm free from pain,
And I rarely do things wrong.

If a problem ever comes my way,
I know exactly what to do.
I give the problem to a thing
That I brought home from the zoo.

It's small and scaly, green and red,
And lives beneath my floor.
And I feed it all my problems,
Which it eats, then asks for more.

With this munching, hungry monster,
Devouring all my woes,
I appear to be quite calm and staid
And intimidate my foes.

But if you think this strange, then wait!
Just listen, 'cause there's more.
The thing grew bigger every day
Until it broke out through my floor.

The thing's two horns stuck out. They did!
They stuck up through the floor.

So I had to keep them covered,
Which was not an easy chore.

People wondered and they stared
'Cause the thing got larger still.
And it had an odor you could smell
About a mile on down the hill.

But I kept on. I kept it hid
And fed it all my woes.
So it got huge and huger yet.
Would it ever stop? Who knows?

Then finally it happened,
As you will shortly see.
That hungry, scaly monster
Lunged up and swallowed me.

Now I *really* have problems.

The Teddy Preacher

My mom gave me a Teddy,
But it's not what you suppose.
This Teddy is a preacher,
Not a bear with button nose.
My Teddy Preacher looks like Dad,
The leader of our church.
But Dad is gone four nights a week
Running meetings from his perch.
I hug my Teddy (he's nice and soft),
Then I slip from bed and kneel.
I thank my God, but then I say,
"Couldn't Teddy's arms be real?"

ODD-SERVATIONS

An Inside Look at the First Church

of Especially Swell People, Reformed*

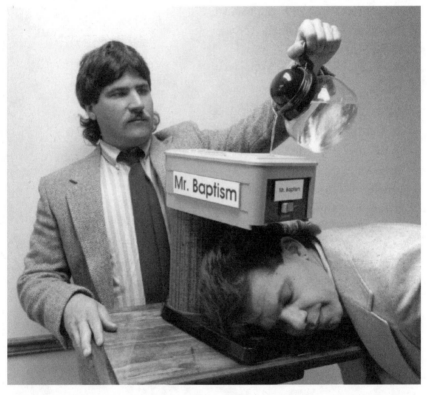

Russ Milhouse's "Mr. Baptism" idea lasted for a week before our leaders declared it "the year's dumbest innovation."

* Photos courtesy of Bud Kelso, First Church photographer.

In the nineteenth century, when horses ruled the roads, our church's founding fathers pioneered the concept of bumper stickers—only they called them "rumper stickers."

The church recently decided that newlyweds Claudia and Jethro Kraft desperately needed a vacation from the youth ministry when they followed the traditional "you may kiss the bride" with "you may *noogie* the groom."

Halloween is a difficult time of year for many Christians, with people going around dressed up as devils and ghosts. That's why our church provides an alternative. Kids dress up in masks that resemble the Sunday school superintendent, and when they approach the doors of fellow churchgoers, they shout, "Trick or *teach!*" If a churchgoer does *not* sign up as a Sunday School teacher on the spot, the kids soap the person's windows. What better way to enlist new teachers?

Our Halloween festivities also allow us to get rid of all of the green-bean casserole left over from various potlucks. Not only do churchgoers put delicious casseroles in the bags of trick-or-teachers, but kids get to "bob for green beans" at the church's harvest-time party.

REAL LIFE

The Day the Church Camp Disappeared

On a Monday afternoon a church camp director and his maintenance director entered the Twilight Zone.

Or so it seemed.

It all started on a Sunday when the camp director, whom I will call Jim, and the maintenance director, Frank, left camp to tend to business at their church.

On Monday morning, Frank and Jim drove back to camp together. When they arrived they found the church van butted up against a tree. The motor was still running, but there was no one inside the vehicle.

Stranger yet, a small motorboat was making circles in the lake, but nobody was in the boat. A few kayaks bobbed gently on the surface of the water. All were unoccupied.

In fact, the entire camp was unoccupied. Totally deserted.

Mystified is a mild way to describe their puzzlement. Entering the main cabin provided no solutions, just more mysteries. The stove was hot and a pot of water was boiling over. Water running in the kitchen sink was dribbling over the edge and forming a puddle on the floor.

Piles of clothes lay everywhere. But it wasn't a haphazard scattering of clothes. Each pile made a complete set—shoes, socks, pants, and shirt, as if the person wearing them had suddenly been sucked out by a cosmic vacuum cleaner.

Venturing into the camp office, Frank and Jim found the electric typewriter still humming and a piece of paper still in place. The words on the paper ended in mid-sentence.

"It looks like there was some sort of natural disaster," Jim said, glancing around. "Where is everyone?"

Jim and Frank didn't say the word *rapture* to each other, but both must have been thinking about the passages of Scripture that speak about what will happen at the end of time when Jesus calls his followers to heaven.

Just then Jim and Frank heard a voice calling to them. The voice belonged to a lone junior-high kid who was wandering around.

"Where is everyone!" the kid exclaimed. "They were here one minute, and then they were gone!"

The sole survivor, if that's an appropriate way to describe him, was a junior-high student who hadn't been sure what to make of the Christian life. Throughout the week he had displayed plenty of skepticism about Jesus, and plenty of people had been praying for him. If Jim and Frank feared that the rapture had occurred without them, the news that this boy was the only one left in camp probably didn't calm those fears.

"Are you sure you don't know where everyone went?" Jim asked. "Was there some sort of emergency?"

In a stunned sort of way, the kid suggested that they look for his friend Tom at the trampoline. "That's where I last saw him."

But the trampoline site was quiet too. Tom's clothes were all that remained, lying on the ground beside the trampoline.

In fact, the outdoors was dotted with mounds of clothing. By the drinking fountain, for instance, they found a T-shirt draped over the bubbler. The shorts and shoes that went with the T-shirt were underneath the fountain.

This was too much. Jim strode to the camp office and phoned the church. Maybe the pastor had some notion of what was going on.

But the pastor had no words of comfort. "Gee, Jim, I don't know where everyone could be. I'm wondering where everyone here at church went. They were in the office a few minutes ago."

Jim placed a call to his wife at work next. When the secretary answered, she said, "That's strange. She was at her desk a second ago, but she's not there now."

For the next half hour, Jim, Frank, and the junior-high boy meandered through camp, checking cabin after cabin. But there was no sign of life.

The Bible says that when heaven gives the signal for the Second Coming, angels will gather people from the four winds and people will start vanishing—maybe popping like soap bubbles, while their spirits zip to the clouds. Could Frank and Jim have missed such a signal?

"Could there have been some national emergency?" Jim wondered.

In the twinkling of an eye, Jim received an answer. He heard a signal. But not from heaven. And it wasn't the sound of an angel's trumpet. It was the sound of a bell coming from somewhere on the campground.

Within two minutes, Frank and Jim were surrounded by one hundred giggling junior-high kids and their fearless leaders who were eager to relate the details of how they had successfully pulled off the ultimate practical joke.

A camp leader with a walkie-talkie in hand had been hiding in the bushes when Frank and Jim drove through the main entrance. Going by the code-name "Rapture-1," this leader radioed back to camp and alerted the second leader, "Rapture-2," that Frank and Jim were on their way. "Rapture-2" rang a bell to alert all campers to go into action. Then, with efficiency that would make a general proud, one hundred kids scattered to predetermined hiding places.

Some crawled underneath cabins. Some jumped in the lake and hid beneath overturned boats. Others hid underneath the dock.

The "rapture scenery" had already been set up—the van against the tree, the boiling water, the overflowing sink, the running typewriter, and the kayaks. The motorboat had been anchored to the bottom of the lake to make it go in circles.

Guessing that the camp director would call back to the church, the leaders who hatched this plot had the presence of mind to inform the pastor of their practical joke and get him to play along.

When Jim called his wife, it was a coincidence that she was away from her desk. As an added coincidence, the secretary just happened to say the ominous words, "That's strange. She was at her desk a second ago, but she's not there now."

According to Frank, he and Jim didn't suspect a practical joke. The idea that camp leaders could coordinate one hundred crazy junior-high kids in such an elaborate plan just didn't occur to them. A natural disaster seemed a more likely possibility.

As you can see, this church camp in northern Illinois had the benefit of being staffed with a highly creative team of leaders. Which goes to show . . . If you have creative leaders on staff, be thankful.

But also be forewarned.

REAL LIFE

Be Composed?

Some people said that Peter Cartwright had the strength to wear out a dozen threshing machines. He was of medium height and packed plenty of power into his two-hundred-pound body. He had a dark complexion and hair as unruly as the wilderness. In fact, Cartwright made his living in the wilderness, spreading the Gospel during the 1800s in what was then considered "the West."

In some ways, Cartwright was like another man of the wilderness, John the Baptist. Both were as blunt as a hammer. As a staunch Methodist, however, Cartwright probably wouldn't be too happy seeing the word "Baptist" associated with his name. According to his autobiography, he was forever debating Baptists and others on the issue of baptism.

Cartwright also didn't think too highly of Easterners, who, he said, were too cultured for their own good. Take the case of a fellow he described as a "fresh, green, live Yankee from down East."

This Yankee, a recent seminary graduate, was well-stocked on theology and had been sent to the region where Cartwright was a circuit-riding preacher. As Cartwright explained, the Yankee thought Westerners were about as primitive as they come—on the same level as cannibals. As for Methodist ministers, the Yankee thought they were illiterate ignoramuses of inferior tact and talent.

Cartwright allowed the green Yankee to preach one night at a camp meeting. But Cartwright was not impressed. He said the Yankee read his sermon, balking, hemming, and coughing the whole way through.

Later in the service, while Cartwright tended to people who were heading for the mourner's bench, a large man was suddenly arrested by the power of God. The man stood to his feet and cried aloud for mercy, which evidently struck the Yankee visitor as an unseemly way to behave.

The little Yankee preacher pressed through the crowd, reached up, tapped the large man on the shoulder and said, "Be composed. Be composed."

When Cartwright saw what was going on, his assessment of the Yankee fell even further. Yelling as loudly as he could, Cartwright called to the large mourner, "Pray on, brother! Pray on! There's no composure in hell or damnation!"

Still, the little Yankee minister kept tapping the large man, saying calmly, "Be composed; be composed, brother."

While making his way through the crowd, Cartwright once again countered with his view. "Pray on, brother! Pray on!"

Reaching the large man, Cartwright took him by the arm to escort him to the mourner's bench, the place prepared for people moved by the Spirit. But the crowd blocked his way, so Cartwright released the man's arm while he cleared a path.

When he did that, the large man began to *really* let loose with what Cartwright called "an ecstasy of joy." In fact, the large man was so overcome with emotion that he attempted to grab Cartwright in a holy hug.

"Fortunately for me, two men were crowded into the aisle between him and myself, and he could not reach me," Cartwright said. "Missing his aim in catching me, he wheeled around and caught my little preacher [the Yankee] in his arms, and lifted him up from the floor; and being a large, strong man, having great physical power, he jumped from bench to bench, knocking the people against one another on the right and left, front and rear, holding up in his arms the little preacher.

"The little fellow stretched out both arms and both feet, expecting every moment to be his last, when he would have his neck broken. O! how I desired to be near this preacher at that moment, and tap him on the shoulder, and say, 'Be composed; be composed, brother!'"

There's a time for composure. I'm all for it. And I realize that leaders need to keep a church under control. But they need to remember whose control it should be under. A church should be kept under God's control, not the leaders' control. When leaders confuse the two, they sometimes make the inadvertent mistake of keeping the Holy Spirit "under control" too. All in the name of maintaining composure.

Most of us probably wouldn't have expected that little Yankee preacher to maintain composure when he was being bounced around like a rag doll. Why, then, should we expect people to maintain perfect composure when the Holy Spirit has them in a holy hug?

Loosen up, brother. Loosen up.

ORIGINS

St. Patrick's Day. Patrick, Ireland's most famous church leader, was not Irish. He was born in the British Isles sometime between A.D. 385 and 460. St. Patrick's Day, March 17, marks the date of his death.

When Patrick was sixteen, raiders kidnapped him and took him to Ireland, where he was forced to work as a shepherd. After six years he had a dream in which a voice told him, "Thy ship is ready for thee." He decided the message meant that he was to run away. Which he did. Patrick fled to the coast, two hundred miles away, where he encountered a ship about ready to sail.

Patrick and the sailors eventually landed in western Europe. But once again Patrick was made a slave—this time by the sailors. So he had to make another escape before he eventually found his way home.

Back home, he began to have visions again. He heard the voice of the Irish people calling him, "Come hither and walk among us." Patrick decided this meant he should return to Ireland. Which he did. And he brought Christianity to the Emerald Isle.

According to legend, Patrick also introduced the Irish symbol of the shamrock. While preaching one day, he used a three-leaf clover—one leaf with three parts—to demonstrate the concept of the Trinity.

The Trinity. Believe it or not, it *is* possible for leaders to get things done at church meetings. The Council of Nicaea in 325 is a good example. It was one of the most important of all councils because this is where the church developed the Nicene Creed—the creed that established the doctrine of the Trinity.

Although the word "Trinity" is never mentioned in the Bible, church leaders argued that the concept of three-in-one is found throughout Scriptures. One of the classic examples is Matthew 28:19, where Jesus says, "Therefore go and make disciples of all nations, baptizing them in the name of the Father and of the Son and of the Holy Spirit . . ."

What's nice about the doctrine of the Trinity is that all Christians today agree on it. So it goes to show that miracles can even occur at church meetings.

St. Nick. One church leader who attended the Council of Nicaea was Nicholas, or good old St. Nick, as we know him now.

St. Nicholas, the patron saint of Russia, was known for his generosity. Legend has it that St. Nicholas dropped pieces of gold down a chimney and into a stocking left hanging there to dry. Three sisters, who were servants, used the gold to escape slavery. To celebrate his generosity, the church in Russia, Holland, and Belgium started the tradition of giving gifts to children on St. Nicholas' feast day—December 6.

Dutch settlers in America brought with them stories of Saint Nick, which they pronounced as "Santa Niklaus." This name was then transformed to Santa Claus and his feast day was changed to December 25.

The popular picture of Santa Claus—beard, pipe, and red clothes—came from Clement Moore, a professor of theology at New York Theological Seminary. In 1823, he wrote *The Visit of St. Nicholas,* also known as *The Night Before Christmas.*

THE FOURTH DAY

And Then There Were Congregations, Governing Day and Night

And God said, "Let there be lights in the expanse of the sky to separate the day from the night, and let them serve as signs to mark seasons and days and years, and let them be lights in the expanse of the sky to give light on the earth." And it was so. God made two great lights—the greater light to govern the day and the lesser light to govern the night. He also made the stars. God set them in the expanse of the sky to give light on the earth, to govern the day and the night, and to separate light from darkness. And God saw that it was good. And there was evening, and there was morning—the fourth day.

GENESIS 1:14–19

In God's infinite wisdom, he created the proper balance between night and day. This balance is represented by the two great creations, the sun and moon, which govern the day and night.

In churches throughout history there has been a similar attempt to find balance—a balance of power between two other great creations, the minister and the congregation.

To create a balance, many churches have developed a system of checks and balances like we have in our government. The only problem is that some churches think a check-and-balance system means that the congregation reminds the minister that they pay his *checks* so he'd better examine his bank *balance* before saying anything that offends them.

As you can see, keeping things in balance is no easy task. It is complicated even more by the complexity of a congregation, which is made up of people of all sizes, shapes, races, and ages. People such as . . .

Singles

Noah's ark didn't have a singles group aboard, and ever since then churches have been notoriously couples-oriented. This has left many singles feeling like outsiders. But as one minister tells me, "I don't mean to stir up feelings of rejection. I love all of my church members, no matter if they are black or white, single or married. I enjoy single

people. Some of my best friends are single. I just wouldn't want my daughter to marry one."

On the positive side, the church provides a way for singles to become couples. An additional benefit is that trying to spot new romantic relationships is one of the best ways to keep people from falling asleep during a dull sermon.

To spot a romance in the making, try using the "hymn and her" system. It enables you to evaluate a relationship by looking at the way couples hold their hymnals. For example:

A probable relationship: The girl is looking at a hymnal held by a guy she is not related to . . . or vice versa, even though there is another hymnal in the rack in front of her.

A definite relationship: The girl is not only *looking* at the guy's hymnal, she's *holding* one side of it while he grips the other side.

A serious dating relationship: While singing hymns, the girl and guy continually glance at each other and smile, just like Sonny and Cher used to do while singing "I Got You, Babe."

A possible marriage: The girl and guy are actually singing "I Got You, Babe" to each other while the rest of the congregation sings "O Come, All Ye Faithful."

Married couples

Speaking of marriage, some of the most distracting people in a congregation are newly married couples engaging in PDA—Public Display of Affection. However, PDA in church is more than distracting. It can also be humiliating to older couples who suddenly realize that the last time they held hands during a service a Democrat was president.

Children

The group responsible for keeping parents so busy that they have no time for PDA is, of course, children.

One of my pet peeves regarding children and the church has to do with Sunday school organization. In most churches, Sunday school classes are organized according to age groups. While this may be an easy system, it doesn't take into consideration different stages of development. Therefore, I propose that churches group children in Sunday school this way:

- Kids who slide under the table.

- Kids who crawl on top of the table and slide across it on their bellies, pretending they are swimming.

- Kids who lean back in their chairs and almost fall over.

- Kids who try to sneak out the door when the teacher is not looking.

- Kids who slouch down in their chairs so low that their heads are the only part of their body touching the back rest.

As most educators will tell you, the teaching process is enhanced if all of the students are in the same vicinity—at least within shouting distance.

With this system, a teacher can be assured that all students will be under the table, on top of the table, or sneaking out the door.

Minorities

Most churches do not consider themselves racist, so why are so many churches segregated? What would happen if predominately white churches started uniting with predominately black churches?

It would be great for everyone except Dick and Jane, who would be out of a job—again.

Dick and Jane are the white, middle-class kids who used to appear in primary school readers, telling their dog Spot to "Run, Spot, run!" That poor dog probably spent three-fourths of every day running around for Dick and Jane. He's probably still seeing a therapist about it.

As for Dick and Jane, they lost their jobs when educators dropped their books from the reading curriculum. The pair quickly found new employment, however, when a publisher of Sunday school curriculum for predominately white churches heard that they were job hunting. Look closely at Sunday school materials and you will see that the Bible characters look like adult versions of Dick and Jane. They just matured a bit and started wearing robes and sandals.

When Dick reached puberty, he grew a beard and started posing as Moses' brother Aaron. It's got to be him because every once in a while, he says, "See the plagues, Pharoah. Plague, Pharaoh, plague! Plague, plague, plague!"

If churches integrate, African-American members will not be too thrilled to see all of the Bible characters looking as white as Ivory soap. So Dick and Jane may find themselves in the unemployment line again. But it's got to be done. It's just one of the sacrifices we'll have to make to integrate.

See Dick and Jane standing in the unemployment line. Stand, Jane, stand.

The Elderly

In television sitcoms, elderly people are generally portrayed as sexually obsessed seniors or grandmothers on motorcycles. I guess TV producers want us to believe that elderly people are nice as long as they act like hormone-crazed teenagers. If they act like elderly people normally act, forget them.

Our youth-oriented bias keeps us from recognizing that elderly people have value because they're unique. They're different from middle-aged folks, who are different from young adults, who are different from teenagers, who are different from just about any life form in the galaxy.

Elderly folks are vital to church life, and as baby-boomers age they're going to make up a larger and larger part of it.

Baby-boomers as senior citizens. A frightening thought.

I'm a baby-boomer, and I'm already sick of hearing about all the great things we supposedly did during the wild and wacky sixties. Imagine what boomers are going to be like when they hit retirement age. If we thought our parents and grandparents went on and on about the Depression, wait'll we start reminiscing about the sixties.

Baby-Boomer Senior Citizen (speaking to his grandchildren): You kids don't appreciate all the modern conveniences you have today. When I was your age, we didn't get to take a bath for weeks at a time.

Grandchild: But Grandpa, you didn't *want* to take a bath. You were a hippie!

Baby-Boomer Senior Citizen: Don't sass me, young'un! I used to walk six miles in a protest line every day, without shoes, even in the snow.

Grandchild: But Grandpa, you *wanted* to walk without shoes. You said shoes were part of the capitalist pig system!

Baby-boomer senior citizens may also re-create sixties fads, but with an elderly twist. They'll replace nursing homes with nursing communes and start painting their liver spots in psychedelic colors. When doctors tell them to provide a specimen for analysis, they'll stage a sit-in in the waiting room and chant, "Heck no! We won't go!"

Ministering to elderly baby-boomers will be a challenge for the younger generation. But we'll survive—as long as nobody tries to bring back the word *groovy*.

NEWS IN THE PEWS

JANUARY

The Official Newsletter of the
First Church of Especially Swell People, Reformed

"The friendly church where even the pastor's wife feels accepted"

Head Pastor:
The Extremely Reverend Bobo Hixson

Assistant Pastor:
The Very Reverend Sammy Smitt

Youth Pastors:
The Rarely Reverend Jethro and Claudia Kraft

Recovering

Let's pray for Clifford Spangle, who was injured while being baptized in Lake Onion last week. He was knocked unconscious when yours truly, Pastor Bobo, tried to immerse him through 6 feet of ice on the frozen lake. (Note: The doctor says Clifford will be seeing double for another week, so if you want to send him a dozen flowers, save money and only send six.)

Pastor Bobo's Chat

WELL, OUR GOOD FRIEND Mr. New Year has arrived again, and with it comes many resolutions. I, for one, am happy to report that our church's "Kick that Filthy Habit" course is helping people keep their resolution to give up smoking. Jean Osmand tells me that in just one day, our program helped her cut down from four packs a day to only three cigarettes per day.

Granted, each of those three cigarettes is over 25 feet long and takes roughly a third of a day to smoke. But let's give Jean a hand for her effort anyway. She says the three cigarettes are great, as long as you don't mind asking somebody in the next room to light your cigarette and tap off your ashes.

Have a wonderful New Year, my sheep.

Your Shepherd,

Pastor Bobo

Rev. Bobo Hixson

Play Auditions

Anyone interested in coming out for the new winter play should call Tom and Jennifer Brock. The play is called "Gulliver's Ministries." It's about a devout pastor who wants to do something exciting for the Lord but suddenly wakes up to find his hands tied by dozens of small church committees.

Nursery Notes

Nursery workers, please, please, *please* try to keep the screaming and crying down to a reasonable level. We've had complaints that you're bothering the babies.

Missions Report

Next week, the Missions Committee will meet to decide whether to drop a first-aid relief package into Howard Livingstone's camp. The kit should come in handy because Howard's assistant was hurt badly when a falling relief package hit him in the head two months ago.

Eye Tests for Prophets

Do you think you might be a prophet? If so, you will want to stop in at the church next week. Pastor Sammy has devised an eye test for prophets. He holds a blank eye-chart in front of a prophet and asks him to read, from left to right, the letters that are *going* to be printed there.

More On Our Creche Scene

Good news! The city decided we can put up our creche scene in front of city hall again next Christmas. But there is one stipulation. With the creche scene, we have to include the statue of an ACLU lawyer handing a court summons to one of the shepherds.

Clown Ministry

The clown ministry will no longer perform during Sunday services because too many people were confusing it with Pastor Bobo's sermons.

Congratulations!

Congratulations to Dave and Jan Yoke on the birth of their new baby boy, Jimbo. Dave and Jan gave birth using the controversial Leboyer method. With Leboyer, a baby is delivered in semi-darkness, thereby preventing the baby from being traumatized by light and allowing the doctor to leave unnoticed for a smoke.

Dave and Jan also used the hospital's birthing room, which was specially designed to be like home. Six screaming kids tore through the room; the sound of neighbors fighting and the phone ringing was piped in through a state-of-the-art sound system; and Jehovah's Witnesses knocked on the door at the most inconvenient times.

Cassette Tapes

Anyone wishing to obtain cassette tapes of the Sunday services should contact Bud Kelso. Tapes are available in three forms:

Regular taped version—$1.50

Speeded-up version so the pastor sounds like a chipmunk—$4.50

Backwards version for Minnesota-raised Lutherans who want the pastor to sound Swedish—$6.00

More Congrats!

Our hearty congratulations to eight-year-old Spiff Johnson who completed a year of perfect Sunday school attendance by showing up in December even though he had measles, chicken pox, and malaria.

Prayer Requests

Please pray for an end to the epidemic of measles, chicken pox, and malaria afflicting our church youth.

Vital Statistics

Average Church Attendance as Tabulated By the National Association of People Who Count By Twos: 298

Total Offering: $3.50

Loose Change Found in Pew Cushions: $75.00

ODD-SERVATIONS

*An Inside Look at the First Church of Especially Swell People, Reformed**

You know the problem: The wife and kids go to church while the husband stays home and reads the newspaper. But in our congregation, if the husband won't go to church, we bring the church to the husband! Meeting in Bo Grober's bedroom, this worship team sings the familiar chorus: "Someone's reading the sports page Lord, Kumbaya! Someone's reading the sports page Lord, Kumbaya! Someone's reading the sports page Lord, Kumbaya! Oh, Lord! Bo knows church."

* Photos courtesy of Bud Kelso, First Church photographer.

Some people believe this out-of-focus photo of the baptismal is conclusive evidence that the Loch Ness Monster attends the First Church of Especially Swell People, Reformed. They say our church needs to improve its outreach to newcomers because the Loch Ness Monster attended for two years before anyone even noticed.

"I'm convinced that Nessie attends our church," says one oldtimer. "Who else would've called the church office last week saying that he was interested in a singles group because all the girls he used to know are now extinct?"

To bait the beast, Pastor Sammy recently arranged for 350 pounds of raw meat to be placed with coffee and donuts on the hospitality table after Sunday service.

Unfortunately, Miss Kenny's sixth grade Sunday school class devoured the meat before anyone could find out if the lure worked.

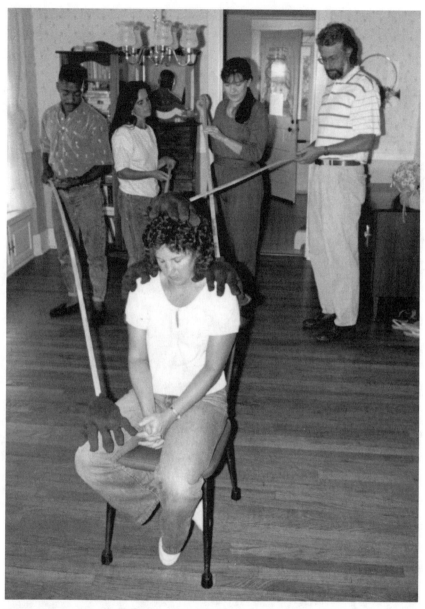

First Church members have a lot of faith when it comes to praying for the healing of sick friends. We just don't have much faith when it comes to contagious illnesses. That's why we keep our distance when laying on hands.

Miss Kenny's sixth grade Sunday school class got a bit out of hand when they re-enacted the destruction of Sodom and Gomorrah in what used to be the church's educational wing.

REAL LIFE

Man Cannot Live by Mammon at All

I have yet to see anyone get up in front of church and start singing, "Mammon! How I love ya, how I love ya, my dear old Mammon!" When we compromise with Mammon, we usually do it in much more subtle ways. One way is to cater to the rich members of our churches—the people who pay the salaries and make that new educational wing possible.

It's very natural. It's also very nasty.

I get excited whenever the church makes it clear that there is no difference between a prince and a pauper in the eyes of heaven. That's why I like the true story revolving around the death of Franz-Josef I, ruler of the Austro-Hungarian empire—a story that I tell in verse (with apologies to Dr. Seuss).

The King of Beggars

Franz-Josef was an emperor, endowed with mighty power.
He ruled every home and every farm and every tower.
But powerful or not, every ruler meets his end,
For death is democratic, on that you can depend.

So Franz saw his last as his eyes dissolved to dark,
And his soul swam away like a spirit-world shark.
The Austro-Hungarian leader of this bitter-fisted land
Was laid to rest while other men rose up to take command.

Elaborate, regal funerals have a long and great tradition,

And Franz deserved a ceremony befitting his position.
So this court of distant days assembled all its best
In hats with ostrich feathers, and medals on their chest.

The procession moved along, through torch-enlightened streets
While a band played its dirges to somber, darkened beats.
The coffin was imperial as it moved on through the cold.
Like a treasure chest of death, it was draped in black and gold.

To the monastery gate came this cortege of the king.
And behind the gate stood churchmen in a quiet, careful ring.
Leading the procession was the Marshall of the Court.
He stepped on toward the church, which stood solid like a fort.

Pulling out his sword, he used its hilt to pound the gate,
And his voice commanded "Open!" like a man who wouldn't wait.
But the gates did not respond. They remained secure and strong,
While the air was filled with silence, both dramatic and quite long.

"Who goes there?" boomed a voice, finally speaking for the church.
Then the Marshall cleared his throat. The horses gave a lurch.
The Marshall spoke out clear, the Marshall spoke out loud,
Hoping that his voice would strike awe throughout the crowd.

He said . . .

"We bear the remains of his Imperial and Apostolic Majesty, Franz-
Josef I, by the Grace of God Emperor of Austria, King of Hungary,
Defender of the Faith, Prince of Bohemia-Moravia, Grand Duke of
Lombardy, Venezia, Styrgia . . ."

On and on went the roll call of titles, honors, claims.
Thirty-seven titles named, wrapped in glory, framed in fame.
But the gates did not respond. They did not open wide.
And the coffin remained stranded, with mourners at its side.

At last, the church responded. It said, "We know him not."
"Who goes there?" it then added, as if it had forgot.

So the Marshall spoke again. He announced a shorter name.
He gave two titles for his king. Two titles' worth of fame.

He said . . .

"We bear the remains of his Majesty, Franz-Josef I, Emperor of
  Austria and King of Hungary."

That's all the Marshall said. Two titles, nothing more.
But still the gates were quiet. Quiet to the core.
"We know him not," said the church, a second time that day.
"Who goes there?" said the church, without hesitation or delay.

Everyone was silent while the Marshall thought a while.
Then he raised his head and scratched his beard and broke out in a
  smile.
When "Who goes there?" was repeated with the firmness of a rock,
The Marshall knew which words would open every lock.

He said . . .

"We bear the body of Franz-Josef, *our brother, a sinner like us all.*"

Then the gates opened wide, and the coffin moved within,
For our Lord had stretched his arms to cover every sin.
His arms closed around this king, a beggar, one who's poor.
For he had left his titles in a trash heap by the door.

REAL LIFE

The Eternal Community

Milo Kaufmann once taught Sunday school in a sheltered-care home for sixteen to twenty older men. The woman who ran the home was, as Milo put it, "a canny, middle-aged Irish woman."

Milo and this woman often swapped stories after Sunday school. One of the woman's most striking memories was of an incident that happened when she was ten years old.

It was early in the morning, the woman recalled, when she woke up to a sight that would stay with her no matter how many years went by, no matter how many other memories crowded her mind. At the foot of the bed were three shining figures wearing robes that looked as if they had been sewn from the fabric of the sun.

The girl was in her mother's bed, so she turned to awaken her mother. But the woman was already awake, her eyes fixed on the remarkable visitors.

"Don't be afraid," her mother said. "Those three are angels."

She and her mother believe the angels were sent to comfort them, for their presence *did* comfort them when, three days later, the girl's father died.

✳ ✳ ✳

When we think of our congregations, we usually forget that our fellowship extends beyond the visible world. We forget that the Christian family isn't restrained by the boundaries of our material universe. We rarely stop to think that it includes seraphim, cherubim, archangels, and an entire host of saints awaiting us in heaven.

My friend Milo related this story of the angels in a book called *Heaven: A Future Finer Than Dreams.* In the same book, he points out a critical difference between Eastern religions and Christianity. In many Eastern religions, the underlying goal is to attain *unity,* to achieve union, to lose individuality, to dissolve self into some sort of cosmic soup. But the brilliance of Christianity is that the primary goal is to seek *communion,* not *union.* We seek community, both in this life and beyond this life. Our relationships extend into eternity; they are not dissolved by the infinite.

Our relationships may be changed, of course. For instance, the pain and alienation that exist between parent and child will be resolved in heaven. The relationship will be transformed, but not eliminated.

Relationship is what this life is about. It's also what the afterlife will be about.

"The God of Israel and of the church is primarily concerned about loving community, and loving conversation between man and God," Milo writes. "You and I, as persons, will be held forever distinct in the loving regard of God himself."

Perhaps heaven will bring about the same feeling I get when I return from vacation. When I open the door to our house after a long trip, the place seems different. There is a strangeness and yet a comfortable familiarity about being home.

When I enter the gates of heaven, I think this same feeling will be there, only heightened and sharper. There will be a strangeness to heaven but also a comfortable familiarity. I'll be home.

Let people call heaven "pie in the sky." That's okay. I don't mind. It will be the best pie I've ever tasted.

ORIGINS

Haloes. The halo didn't have a very saintly origin. It started out as a pagan symbol, a radiance that encircled the head of a god. Eventually, the halo became a religious symbol for Christians, even though certain leaders in the early church were upset by its pagan origins.

Some historians say that one of the reasons halos became popular is because they made a handy way to protect statues. By placing wood or brass circular disks over the heads of statues in the seventh century, the statues were protected from rain, erosion, and bird droppings.

The word *halo* comes from "halos," which is a Greek word that means "circular threshing floor." Farmers threshed grain by laying it on the ground and then driving oxen in a circle over the grain.

Tithe. Abraham and Jacob pioneered the concept of the tithe—giving one-tenth of their earnings to God. Abraham was the first person in the Bible to practice tithing when he gave "a tenth of everything" to the mysterious high priest Melchizedek. Jacob decided to give God one-tenth of his earnings (Genesis 28:22), and in return, he asked God to protect him during the trip back to his father's house.

Worship. Before the fourteenth century, the word *worship* was spelled "worthship." "In a sacred place men get a feeling of worth," notes Charles Ferguson in *A is for Advent*.

Carolers and Nativity Scenes. Francis of Assisi is often credited with two of the most famous Christmas traditions—caroling and nativity scenes.

Although nativity scenes could be found in earlier years, Francis popularized the tradition in 1223 or 1224. His may have been one of the first outdoor nativities. It even made use of live animals.

Francis encouraged the townspeople to gather around the nativity scene and sing gospel songs. Many believe this was the start of Christmas caroling. Prior to this, most Christmas hymns were deadly serious and sung in Latin. Francis brought Christmas music to the common people.

THE **FIFTH** DAY

Let the Land Teem with Church Buildings

And God said, "Let the water teem with living creatures, and let birds fly above the earth across the expanse of the sky." So God created the great creatures of the sea and every living and moving thing with which the water teems, according to their kinds, and every winged bird according to its kind. And God saw that it was good. God blessed them and said, "Be fruitful and increase in number and fill the water in the seas, and let the birds increase on the earth." And there was evening, and there was morning—the fifth day.

GENESIS 1:20–23

Birds arrived on the fifth day of creation, and you can be sure it wasn't long before they started building nests. You know it's nest-building time when you see birds flitting from branch to branch with twigs and string in their beaks.

And you know it's church-building time when you see ushers flitting from pew to pew with collection plates in their beaks. You'll need a lot of ushers when you begin a building program because you'll be taking a lot of special offerings. Birds can make a nest out of just about anything, but people need lots of cash. That's why a church shouldn't hop into a building project without first deciding whether a structure is

115

really necessary. After all, in Moses' day the Israelites had no building. They were nomads, traveling throughout the desert, living in one spot for a short time, then pulling up the tent stakes and moving on. It must have been a real pain to lug around fifty camel-loads of Sunday school materials, let alone the overhead projectors. So why did they do it?

My theory is that the Israelites knew how terrible it was to be slaves to someone else's building projects—that of the Pharoah in Egypt—so they weren't too excited about becoming slaves to their own. Also, Moses was probably afraid that if he left Aaron in charge of the building committee, he would have them dancing around a golden air-conditioning unit.

If after evaluating all the pros and cons your church does decide to begin a building program, you will need to form a building committee. Keep in mind that this committee can serve a function far more important than that of making decisions about construction. Used correctly, a building committee can radically reduce your utility bills. The heat

generated during church building committee arguments can keep your church cozy all winter. By keeping as few as four committee members in your furnace, the bickering will generate so much heat that people will be able to attend church in gym shorts no matter how cold the weather gets.

You can also equip your furnace with a special thermostat. When the temperature starts to cool, it automatically drops a remodeling plan in front of the building committee members and the heat goes on.

Know Your Personality

Church buildings reflect the personality of the congregation and denomination. The following design ideas will help you build an edifice that fits your church:

For the church where everyone tries to sit in the back row and nobody ever sits in the front rows.

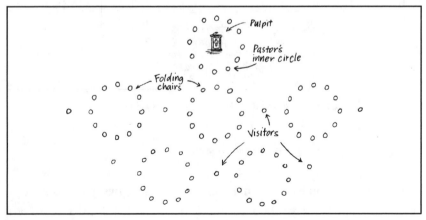

For the church in which people tend to form cliques.

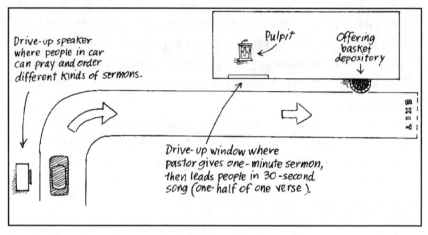

For the church in a hurry—a building modeled after fast-food restaurants.

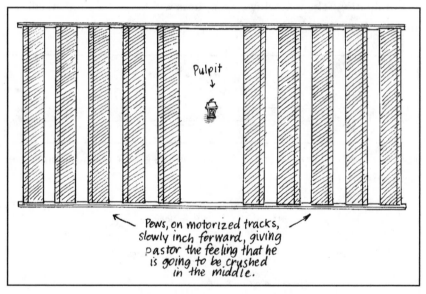

For the church that is divided into two opposing factions.

Learning from the Past

Every generation leaves its mark on church buildings. (For instance, my sixth-grade Sunday school class left approximately 15,643 marks on our church building.) The following review of distinctive features of church buildings throughout history will give you an appreciation for the past and ideas for the present.

Domes. A lot of medieval churches had fancy domes covered with heavenly art work. To focus their attention on heaven, churchgoers simply glanced upward. Some twentieth-century churches have adapted this idea by using the dome to flash football scores and game highlights. This has increased male attendance by 150 percent.

Statues. When the Reformation took place, Protestant churches rid buildings of statues. But with the dwindling attendance in some denominations today, statues are making a comeback. Ministers are putting statues in their pews to give the church a filled-up look, thus improving morale. In some of these churches the statues show more emotion than the people.

Flying Buttresses. Flying buttresses are elegantly designed braces that relieve pressure on the walls of Gothic cathedrals. They should not be confused with walking buttresses or couch-potato buttresses.

Baptismal Fonts. In churches where infant baptism is practiced, the baptismal font is often a small basin. In churches where adult immersion is common, the baptismal font is large. And in churches where there is no air-conditioning, the baptismal font is eliminated altogether. People sweat so much that they leave church looking as if they have been fully immersed.

Pulpits. Many churches have started breeding a new type of dog called the "pulpit bull." This vicious guard dog is specially trained to attack people who try to add spontaneity to a service by going up to the pulpit and sharing their thoughts when they haven't been scheduled to do so.

Spires. In the past, church spires pointed to the sky to remind the world of higher things. Today, some church spires point at the offering basket to remind parishioners that they still owe $4 million on the mortgage.

Examine these ideas carefully, discuss them with your fellow churchgoers, and then draw your own conclusions. Or, if you prefer, take photographs of your own conclusions.

Some Final Considerations

When people are hunting for a house, realtors tell them that the three most important considerations are location, location, and loca-

Pulpit Bull

tion. Churches need to be concerned about location too; but in contrast to most homebuyers, their goal should *not* be to avoid impoverished areas. About the only location a church might want to avoid is the backyard of a nuclear power plant. But even this is controversial. Testifying before Congress, one member of a Methodist church said, "Our church has been located next to a nuclear power plant for over twenty years, and I have suffered *no* psychological or physical effects."

However, he did receive strong disagreement from his other head.

IF WE BUILD IT, THEY WILL COME

When we started our building project at the First Church of Especially Swell People, Reformed, we made a point of involving everyone. We even went as far as to invite people to submit their own designs, knowing this would give them a sense of "ownership." We also knew it would give the building committee an evening of entertainment, hooting at all the silly ideas.

As it turned out, we were wrong. The designs provided an entertaining *week*. Here are a some of the best.

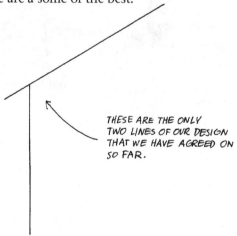

THESE ARE THE ONLY TWO LINES OF OUR DESIGN THAT WE HAVE AGREED ON SO FAR.

Design by: The building committee. Their motto: "Give us another three months and we'll give you another line."

MINISTER WEARS TRADITIONAL VESTMENTS OF ALL GOLFERS: WHITE SHOES, PURPLE PLAID PANTS AND BRIGHT RED SHIRTS.

CADDY #1 CARRIES GOLF CLUBS.

CADDY #2 CARRIES PULPIT.

CONGREGATION

BAPTISMS ARE PERFORMED WHENEVER MINISTER HITS BALL INTO WATER HAZARD. ALLOWS NEW BELIEVER TO RETRIEVE BALL DURING IMMERSION.

Church of the Almighty 18 Holes

Design by: Pastor Bobo, with assistance by other members of the local Sunday Golfers/Ministerial Association.

Design by: The Sunday school staff. (All exterior walls are covered with industrial-strength flannel graph. This allows you to rearrange cardboard windows and doors, changing the church's appearance week by week.)

Design by: Hank Spatula's Gobs-of-Faith Friday Fellowship Group.

Design by: The Fellowship of Christian Business People Who Travel All the Time and Never Attend Church or Recognize Their Children.

ODD-SERVATIONS

*An Inside Look at the First Church of Especially Swell People, Reformed**

Always on the cutting edge, the First Church of Especially Swell People, Reformed, has tried to make *all* parts of the church accessible to wheelchairs—even the bell tower.

On this day, Pastor Sammy's wheelchair was clocked at speeds reaching 60 miles per hour as he roared down the five-story-high ramp. Fortunately, the parachute that opened up at the back of his wheelchair helped to bring him to a stop before he ran into the side of Danny's Grocery Store one mile down the road.

* Photos courtesy of Bud Kelso, First Church photographer.

Here is Russ Milhouse's answer to roach hotels—roach monasteries. When roaches wander into the monastery, they are required to become celibate, eliminating the problem of bugs multiplying at horrifying rates. Also, monastery roaches are well-behaved. Instead of raiding kitchen food sources, they grow their own garbage in carefully tended gardens. (Available in both Catholic and Protestant "high church.")

Our church—a 150-member congregation—slightly overestimated the size of its new sanctuary. "My pencil must've slipped when I was doing the drawings," said the architect just before he moved out of the country.

After discussing the pros and cons of the new carpeting, the building committee votes unanimously to do something about the level of static electricity in
the church.

REAL LIFE

Walking on Holy Land

Mark Twain thought people exaggerated the beauty of the Holy Land.

According to Twain, the area that one writer described as an earthly paradise really consisted of "an unobtrusive basin of water, some mountainous desolation, and one tree." He also said, "Of all lands there are for dismal scenery, I think Palestine must be the prince." The reason the Israelites considered it a land of milk and honey, he added, was because the only scenery they had viewed for the last forty years had been desert.

But Twain also recognized the reason so many people see beauty in the Holy Land. It's not because the place looks like Shangri-la. It's because of what took place there. And that's true. Whether you're talking about the Holy Land or a church building, it's the events, the history, the people that give it meaning.

I've never been to the First Baptist Church in Montgomery, Alabama. But whether the building is beautiful or not, the events that happened there have created a deep sense of "place" for its members. The building has a sense of beauty.

On May 21, 1963, the Freedom Riders took refuge there. These were the people who stood up against segregation laws. Or, more accurately, they "sat down" against the laws. They dared to take seats on a bus and travel the highways of the South.

Before finding refuge at the First Baptist Church, they had arrived at a deserted Montgomery bus station, only to be ambushed by a crowd of white folks who emerged from numerous hiding places. The Riders were beaten with baseball bats, bottles, and lead pipes by over one hundred people.

Once inside the church the Freedom Riders were protected, but a crowd was gathering outside. At about five o'clock, worshipers started arriving for prayer and song. The following synopsis of what happened is based on information from Taylor Branch's Pulitzer Prize-winning book *Parting the Waters:*

The crowd of white people outside the First Baptist Church grew throughout the evening until many churchgoers became afraid to enter the building. The church's only police protection at this point was a thin band of U.S. marshals.

The reports kept getting worse for the worshipers. The crowd outside was getting bigger. Car windows were being broken. Groups of people started "nigger chants," challenging blacks to come out of the church.

Rev. Martin Luther King, Jr., was one of the people inside. Against the advice of other leaders, he decided to face the crowd, but when he did, stones began to fly. When a cylinder landed at his feet, a fellow preacher, fearing that it was a bomb, snatched it up and tossed it toward a vacant area.

Eight o'clock. The mob overturned a car and an old man tossed a match at it. The car erupted in flames.

"Let's clean the niggers out of here!" someone yelled.

The crowd was edging closer to the church.

Inside the church, people sang hymns.

A brick flew through the air and crashed against the leg of a U.S. marshall, sending him to the ground. Rioters started tossing Molotov cocktails, but most of the homemade bombs were ineffective.

Church leaders kept in touch with a Justice Department official at an Air Force base outside Montgomery. The Justice Department official kept in touch with the attorney general in Washington, D.C. It was the usual political mess, with the federal government and state government bickering over whether Washington could get involved in a state conflict.

U.S. marshals began firing tear gas into the crowd outside the church. Inside, leaders tried to calm people, but some churchgoers started preparing for the worst, bringing weapons into view.

The crowd outside kept growing and moving closer, a mass of almost three thousand people. About fifteen hundred people were inside the church. On top of the church, lookouts watched for help—police or military help. Whatever.

Men with weapons stood at every entrance to the church, ready to defend against the crowd outside.

Reinforcements arrived in the form of more U.S. marshals. More tear gas. The rioting crowd pulled back. Jubilant, the churchgoers sang hymns and lifted prayers of thanks.

But the wind began playing tricks, and the cloud of tear gas moved toward the church, seeping inside the building. Windows were quickly closed, and the packed church became a summer steam box. People panicked. Deacons had to forcibly prevent some people from running out of the church straight into a knot of rioters.

After recovering from the latest volley of tear gas, the crowd outside the church became furious. They moved forward with greater determination, finally reaching the doors.

They smashed sticks against the front doors, snapping wood. Splintering. Cracking. Retreating marshals slipped into the church through back doors.

A brick smashed through the church's stained glass window, hitting an old man in the head.

Children were rushed to the basement.

People were told to lie on the floor.

More stones sailed through the air. Windows all around the church shattered under the rainfall of rocks.

The tear gas continued, but now it entered the building and choked more churchgoers than rioters.

The attorney general put army units in Georgia under alert.

The politicians continued their word-wrestling.

Bullets were fired into four homes of blacks living near the church.

A brick knocked another U.S. marshall to the ground, this one hitting the man's head.

A Justice Department official reported to the attorney general that he thought the next wave of rioters would break into the church.

Just as the attorney general was about to commit troops to stop the riot, the Alabama governor declared a state of martial law. The Alabama police finally responded. So did the Alabama National Guard, bayonets in place.

The crowd dispersed.

A refuge. A place for healing wounds. A place where people can stand against an outside force. That is what the First Baptist Church in Montgomery successfully provided for the Freedom Riders who sought protection there. That is what a church is all about. And that is what makes a church a "place."

This sense of place isn't something you can see. Maybe that's why Mark Twain couldn't fully appreciate the Holy Land until after dark, when the sight of physical landmarks dimmed, giving way to the sight of spiritual landmarks built over centuries of mystery.

"In the starlight," he said, "Galilee has no boundaries but the broad compass of the heavens, and is a theater meet for great events . . . for the birth of a religion able to save a world. . . . One can comprehend it only when night has hidden all incongruities and created a theater proper for so grand a drama."

Real Life

We've Never Been the Same

It was an ordinary year during the Middle Ages, and warriors were doing what they did best—whacking people with their swords. On this particular occasion, the Jutes were whacking the Swedes and conquering their villages.

Peter Gyldenstierne, the Jutes' number-one bully, ordered the people of one Swedish village to assemble in front of the local church. He displayed his sword, maybe did a few demonstrations with it, and then made his demand: "I want those two bells in your church tower. Tell me how to get them down."

Getting no response, Gyldenstierne added a threat. "If nobody tells me how to get the bells from the tower, I will slaughter every one of you!"

The people remained silent.

"Tell me how to get those bells or you're all dead!" he commanded again.

Still no response. Nobody said a word. Not one.

Gyldenstierne let the threat soak into their minds.

He waited.

And it worked. A man finally spoke up.

"I'll show you how to get the bells on one condition: that you agree to provide for my wife and children."

Peter Gyldenstierne agreed. So the villager told him to have his men dig sand from the shore and pile it on the sides of the church's bell tower. When this was accomplished, the villager climbed the tower and cut the bell's chains. The bells fell to the ground unharmed, cushioned by the slope of sand.

Expecting thanks, or at least a grunt of approval, the villager gasped when he heard Gyldenstierne's response. The Jute leader pointed at him and said, "Take him prisoner!"

"But you said—!"

"I said I would provide for your wife and children, and that I will," Gyldenstierne assured him. "As for you . . ."

Gyldenstierne pointed to the church tower where the bells once hung. "You betrayed your town. You'll make a good replacement for the bells."

That day the villager was hanged where the bells once chimed.

Why were the bells so important? Why would an entire village risk extermination for the sake of a couple chunks of music-making metal? Jane Yolen answers these questions in her book *Ring Out!* which tells the story of Gyldenstierne and the bells. Bells, she says, were once considered the soul of a village.

The bells—these unassuming parts of a church building—affected the lives of just about every person in Western Europe during the Middle Ages. When the bells lost their prominence, the repercussions were felt worldwide. We still feel the effects today. We all do.

Church bells managed the rhythm of all of life in a medieval village. Bells signaled when it was time to wake up, when it was time for church, when the city gates were going to open or close, when the market was opening, and when it was time to sleep.

Bells were used to announce births, deaths, victories, and defeats. They even functioned as a newspaper, Yolen says. They pealed whenever there was a fire, invasion, or revolution. In fact, Yolen notes, some bell ringers would use a special code to tell fire fighters which part of the town was burning.

Some villagers even baptized their bells, complete with godparents. They also believed that bells had the power to drive away demons and keep pestilence at bay.

Bells affected lives. But when bells began to lose prominence, lives were affected even more drastically. The clock replaced the bells, and the world hasn't been the same since.

The first clocks had no face; they simply sounded bells every hour. That's why we even have the word *clock*. It comes from the Middle Dutch word *clocke,* which means "bell."

Benedictine monks were the first to popularize the use of clocks. But then merchants took control of the clocks, snatching control of people's lives away from the church, and they broke time into smaller parts—minutes, then seconds.

The people, instead of letting the church calendar continue to govern the rhythm of their lives, slowly gave in to the faster-paced, more regimented schedule of the clock.

But this didn't happen overnight, and it didn't happen without a fight. As Jeremy Rifkin points out in *Time Wars,* medieval craftsmen had been used to setting their own pace. Likewise, farmers had been

used to following the flow of the seasons. They were not used to having their time broken down into minutes. They were not used to the
schedules set up by the increasingly powerful factories.

"The workers so loathed the new time orientation that many factory
owners were simply unable to secure a labor force," Rifkin writes.
"When they did, absenteeism was high and often workers would quit
after just a few short weeks. In many firms, it was not unusual to experience a one hundred percent labor turnover in one year."

Even if a factory owner had a work force, it was difficult to get people used to the idea of arriving on time. "On time" was a new concept
for people, so employers hired "knockers up" whose job was to go
through town and awaken workers. They banged on windows with
long poles and yanked on strings that were attached to the toes of
sleeping workers.

Factory owners also battled the church calendar, which they
thought gave workers too much time off. In South Wales, for instance,
Rifkin says, "Workers were still losing one week in five as late as the
1840s as they took time off to celebrate various calendrical rituals and
events."

In the end, the merchants won the battle over time, of course. We
now take our clocks and watches for granted, and our church bells
serve only a symbolic and aesthetic function. The clocks have made us
considerably more productive, which has its benefits, to be sure. But
when you take a look at your schedule for the next week and the lack
of room for spontaneous play or worship, don't you wonder? . . .

Are we like that poor Swedish villager? When we gave up our church
bells did we give away our souls?

If I had the time, maybe I could find some answers. But I've got a
deadline to meet.

ORIGINS

Pews. The word *pew* comes from the French word *puie,* which means "raised place." In the early years of the United States, some prominent families were allowed to sit in roped-off sections, separate from "the rabble." These "seats of the snobs" were known as pews.

When the church finally realized that this tradition was inane, not to mention unbiblical, it disposed of seats of honor. All benches became known as pews.

In the eighteenth century, certain families were allowed to buy their pews. If the families had box pews, they would sometimes decorate them, even installing armchairs and fireplaces.

Red Doors. Many churches paint their front doors red to symbolize the blood of Christ.

Chapel. Chapel comes from the Latin word *capella,* which means "cloak." According to tradition, the word originated with the story of St. Martin, a Roman soldier who gave his cloak to a beggar dying of cold.

St. Martin's cloak became a relic and was kept in a building that soon took on the cloak's name—*capella*. In France the word became *chapelle,* and in England it was *chapel*. However you pronounce it, a chapel is a cloak of God for poor beggars such as us.

Nave. In the early days of the church when Christians were persecuted, the faithful sometimes met secretly underneath large, overturned boats on the seashore. Over the years, many church architects have tried to re-create this image by designing the sanctuary with a peaked ceiling that resembles an overturned boat. Also, the main part of a church sanctuary came to be called the nave, which is the Latin word for boat. That's where we get our word *navy*.

Sanctuary. In the Middle Ages, many people believed that being in a church guaranteed that they would be protected from harm and filled with the goodness of the Lord. This is where the concept of sanctuary came from. If a criminal sought sanctuary in a church, he could not be arrested. He was protected by God and influenced by goodness.

In the year 600, King Ethelbert of England put the concept of sanctuary into law. But there were restrictions. He stipulated that people could not stay in the sanctuary longer than forty days. When forty days elapsed, they had to confess the crime to the priest and leave the kingdom. They were given a cross and a white robe and sent to the nearest port. The cross and robe signified that they were still protected by sanctuary.

Although the right of sanctuary was sometimes abused, it existed in England until 1623. A secular version of the same concept is practiced today in embassies, which often provide protection.

THE SIXTH DAY

Let Church Programs Be Fruitful and Multiply

So God created man in his own image, in the image of God he created him; male and female he created them. God blessed them and said to them, "Be fruitful and increase in number; fill the earth and subdue it. Rule over the fish of the sea and the birds of the air and over every living creature that moves on the ground.". . . God saw all that he had made, and it was very good. And there was evening, and there was morning—the sixth day.

GENESIS 1:27–28, 31

We all know the story. God created man and woman on the sixth day and placed them in the garden. Man and woman screwed up, and God sent them out of the garden, where they faced suffering, pain, and tough decisions, like which grocery line is moving fastest.

As if to emphasize the trials of life outside of Eden, the next time we encounter a garden of such significance in the Bible, it is a garden of pain. The Garden of Gethsemene.

Life isn't easy. People have lots of needs. And the church has valiantly tried to meet these needs with a multitude of programs—everything from Bible studies and youth campouts to prayer groups and missionary ventures. Amazingly, many of these programs really work, as long as churches don't lose sight of their ultimate goal—to help people.

Support Groups

A lot of people have benefited from church support groups patterned after the Twelve Steps of Alcoholics Anonymous. Twelve Step programs have been created for people with all sorts of problems, and they have even been created for the *children* of people suffering from these problems. But one area has been neglected during the boom in Christian support groups, and it is an area that has been ignored far too long.

I'm talking, of course, about baldness.

To remedy this glaring error, I hereby offer the following Seven Step Program for people coping with over-exposed scalps:

1. We admitted we were powerless over hair loss—that our hairline had become unmanageable.

2. We made a searching and fearless inventory of the bathroom, counting the number of hairs that have collected on the drain, on our brush, and on our comb.

3. We made a decision to turn our will and our lives over to the care of God, who has numbered the hairs on our head and is probably finding it much easier to keep track of what we have left.

4. We humbly asked God to remove our shortcomings and to prevent our toupee from becoming airborne on windy days.

5. We made a list of all family members who have been tempted to make "bald" jokes and became willing to cut them out of our will.

6. We made a firm commitment to watch all reruns of *Kojak*.

7. And to buy the video of *The King and I.*

The Youth Program

In the old days, youth programs were uncommon, children's church was nonexistent, and kids were forced to sit through interminably long adult-oriented church services, their only means of escape being numerous visits to the bathroom. Although this behavior was disruptive to worship services, it did prove one thing: It *is* possible for a human child to have to go to the bathroom forty times in one hour.

Sometime during the twentieth century, children in churches revolted against the lack of youth programs. Inspired by the successful feminist song "I Am Woman, Hear Me Roar," they composed an anthem of their own—"I Am Child, Hear Me Whine." This sparked the beginning of elaborate youth ministries. Very elaborate youth programs. So elaborate in fact that, due to hectic schedules, unrealistic demands, and enormous levels of stress, youth workers spend much of their lives in a state of disorientation. Some can't even remember how long they have been in youth work. If for some odd reason you want to find out, check the following fool-proof guide. It is based on the principle that the length of time in youth ministry is directly linked to opinions about contemporary rock music. For example:

Statement by Youth Worker	Length of Time in Youth Ministry
"I like that song! Crank up the stereo until it's loud enough for hearing-impaired people on Mars to hear!"	5 months
"That's not bad music. Not as good as the music when I was in school, but not bad."	3 years
"You call that music? It sounds like someone trying to sing while sitting in a dentist's chair with his mouth full of cotton balls!"	8 years
"You call that music? It sounds like someone trying to sing while sitting in a dentist's chair with his mouth full of cotton balls *and the dentist drilling huge craters in his teeth!*"	15 years
"You call that music? It sounds like someone trying to sing while sitting in a dentist's chair with his mouth full of cotton balls and the dentist drilling huge craters in his teeth *without giving him novocaine!*"	30 years
"Huh? Sorry, I didn't hear a thing. Let me turn my hearing aid back on."	50 years

Bible Studies

Another mainstay of church programs is the weekly Bible study. Every Bible study group is unique, of course. But they all include a few stock characters:

Character #1—*The person who loves to debate bizarre theological questions.* This guy asks such puzzlers as, "Can a black widow spider devour her husband and still remain submissive?"

Character #2—*The person who hates to debate and wants everyone to agree about everything.* This person wants to devour Character #1.

Character #3—*The person who is afraid to say anything for fear of saying something stupid.*

Character #4—*The person who is NOT afraid to say anything, even stupid things.* This person is sure that when the book of Kings mentions David's concubines, it's talking about farm machinery.

Character #5—*The person who knows the Bible backward and forward.* This person usually provides interesting Bible trivia such as: "Did you know that Hosea's wife, Gomer, is the only wife of a prophet mentioned by name in the Bible?" (The only thing this person *doesn't* know is why Hosea would admit he was married to a woman with a name like Gomer.)

Retreats

Retreats are a wonderful antidote to the everyday stress of life, which is everywhere. In jobs. At home. Even in the church.

One vivid memory I have of church retreats is going on "trust walks." On trust walks, the group splits into pairs. One person in each pair is blindfolded and led around by his or her partner for about fifteen minutes.

Then everyone returns to the big group and the blindfolded person discusses how it felt. The blindfolded person generally says things like, "I really felt vulnerable letting myself be led around blindly. But you know, I really felt a great sense of trust, a real bonding with my partner. And I really got in touch with the texture of my surroundings when my partner put something soft and squishy in my hands and then moved my arm in slow circular motions, around and around, pausing only to let my hand feel the cool water. It was a truly moving experience."

The final step, of course, was for everyone to laugh hysterically when it is revealed that the partner had put a sponge in the person's hand and used it to clean the grodiest part of the latrine.

As you can see, trust walks teach important spiritual lessons, such as, "Only trust God."

Adult Education

Finally we come to the adult education program. If yours is in the doldrums, try offering the following courses. They're sure to put a spark into your curriculum:

Evangelism Outreach to Mafia. This course explains that the best way to evangelize gangsters is to fire three rounds of tracts at them from a passing black sedan. Also, if a converted gangster is part of your evangelism team, be sure he does not dip people's feet in concrete before baptizing them in the Chicago River.

Rich Christians in an Age of Credit Cards. In this hands-on workshop, well-to-do Christians try to cross-breed a camel with a paramecium, hoping to create a camel that can go through the eye of a needle.

Nonviolent Protest 405. Students learn nonviolent protest strategies such as letting their bodies go limp when police drag them away. They also find out that several million two- and three-year-olds have been secretly paid to research and refine this technique whenever their parents want them to go somewhere.

Class dismissed.

IN OTHER WORDS

Things that Go on in Bible Studies and Prayer Groups

Amen-nesia. The tendency to forget to pray for somebody two seconds after you promised to "pray about it."

Biblebolstering. A popular Bible-study strategy in which you set your ideas firmly in place first and *then* find Scripture to back them up.

Forgiveness Wounds. The sharp pain you feel when somebody in the Bible study—a person you thought liked you—asks forgiveness for thinking what an idiot you are.

Goodbookanoia. The paranoid feeling you get when you can't locate a book in the Bible and you're flipping pages back and forth like a maniac and you're sure everyone is thinking how unspiritual you are.

Hand-Anvils. People who lean all their weight on you when they lay hands on you to pray.

Honeyprayer. The most common prayer of engaged couples: "Dear God, I hate to bother you with this, but could you postpone the Second Coming until *after* our honeymoon?"

Itsknown. Any question that has such an easy answer that nobody in the Bible study wants to respond.

Limbosphere. An inaccessible part of the brain where all the Bible verses you've memorized since childhood eventually end up.

Goodbookanoia

Megareader. Any person who actually reads Bible genealogies.

Mega-megareader. Any person who can correctly pronounce half of the names in the genealogies.

Mega-mega-megareader. Any person who would actually know whether or not somebody correctly pronounced half of the names in the genealogies.

Nobadiah. A virus that prevents people from reading or quoting obscure Old Testament books like Obadiah.

Praydaze. The habit of not listening to others pray because you're trying to think up what you're going to pray about when it's your turn.

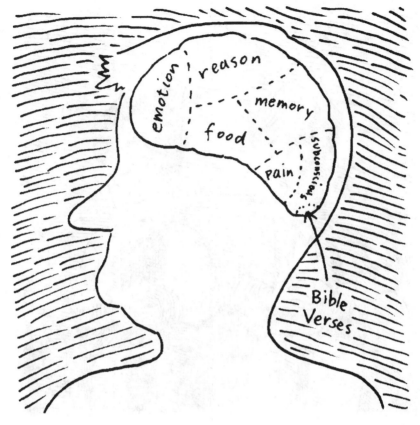

Limbosphere

Prayersertions. Little words like "really" and "just" that people scatter throughout prayers. For example, "I really just want to thank you Lord for just being there when I really needed . . ."

Space Monks. People who avoid praying out loud in a group because they haven't been paying attention and fear they'll repeat what's already been prayed for.

Synchro-eyes. When you open your eyes during group prayer and find yourself looking directly at somebody else who has his or her eyes open.

Synchro-lips. When two people in a prayer group begin praying out loud at the same time.

Synchro-eyes

Synchro-silence. When two people who started praying out loud at the same time simultaneously *stop* praying to let the other person continue.

Synchro-twins. The same two people who (after an uncomfortable silence) both begin praying out loud at the same time again.

Thoughtjams. Traffic jams in your head that prevent your best responses from popping into your mind until you're driving home fifty minutes after the Bible study debate.

How to Conduct Very Short Business Meetings

Meetings have a way of going on and on . . . like creatures in a horror film who just won't die. However, the First Church of Especially Swell People, Reformed, knows how to keep meetings short and sweet. The following minutes may be adapted for use in your own church.

Minutes of the February 6, 1992, meeting of the First Church of Especially Swell People, Reformed, Finance Committee. Members present—Rev. Bobo Hixson, Rev. Sammy Smitt, Clifford Spangle, Dave and Jan Yoke, Karen Omar, Jack Lilly.

7:00 P.M.—Rev. Bobo moved that we begin the meeting.
7:05 P.M.—Nobody seconded the motion.
7:06 P.M.—Meeting was adjourned.

ODD-SERVATIONS

*An Inside Look at the First Church of Especially Swell People, Reformed**

One of the drawbacks of an all-charismatic outfield is that you never know which player is raising his hand to call for the fly ball and which player just feels moved to raise his hand.

* Photos courtesy of Bud Kelso, First Church photographer.

Nick Johnson (left) and Marty Quinn received rave reviews when they played lead roles in the church's hit musical *West Side Sermon*.

In *West Side Sermon*, rival gangs in the same church fight over theological turf. One gang wields chains and overhead projectors and cruises the streets in low-rider church buses. The other gang stands on street corners, dresses in black leather choir robes, and "pitches tithes" against the steps of apartment buildings.

In the climax scene, the two gangs encounter each other while shopping for "praying hands" statues that have brass knuckles on them. This is followed by the hit song "I Feel Petty," which tells how one gang gets offended at everything that members of the other gang propose at church committee meetings.

Do the people in your small group Bible studies disagree about everything? At the First Church, our small groups have *total* unity because they are more than just small groups—they are teeny-weeny groups. As you can see in this photo of Jean Osmand's Bible study, each group has only one person in it. Although group potlucks leave something to be desired, arguments during Bible studies have been totally eliminated, and everybody gets a chance to speak up at meetings. However, attendance is sometimes a problem, so we're thinking of forming even smaller groups, which consist of nobody. That way, if nobody shows up, then there is one hundred percent attendance.

If you've been spiritually uplifted by church handbell choirs, then make room for an innovative "headbell" choir. Pastor Bobo decided that people who sleep in the back row during church can still contribute to the service. Simply attach a bell to their heads. Then, as their sleep-filled heads begin to bob, the bells send out a cheery sound.

REAL LIFE

The Foot Inspector

The Mandarin flicked his fan—an abrupt, direct signal for Gladys Aylward to be quiet. He was unhappy with Gladys because she had failed to find a young girl to serve as a foot inspector for the region.

"Then *you* must be the foot inspector," the Mandarin ordered.

Gladys was stunned. She wasn't Chinese. She was an English missionary. How could she serve as foot inspector? People would never listen to her. Some of them called her a "foreign devil."

But the Mandarin was determined. He explained the job. Gladys would travel throughout the countryside, with the protection of armed guards, and tell villagers about the Central Government's new decree: Footbinding was now illegal. Gladys would inspect the feet of young Chinese girls to make sure their feet were not bound.

Footbinding ranks as one of the most severe traditions ever imposed on women. As recently as the middle of this century, the feet of many young Chinese girls were bound in ten-foot bandages wrapped in such a way that all toes except the big one were pulled underneath the foot. The bandage then was wrapped around the heel so tightly that the sole was drawn as close to the heel as possible. The overall effect was to create a considerably shorter foot.

Howard Levy's book *Chinese Footbinding* provides all of the unpleasant details, including stories of girls who underwent the procedure. One seven-year-old girl tried to hide from her family on the day of her footbinding. But her parents insisted on carrying out the ritual. They found the girl, dragged her home, bound her feet, and commanded her to walk on them.

"My feet felt on fire and I couldn't sleep," the girl said. "On the following days, I tried to hide but was forced to walk on my feet. Mother hit me on my hands and feet for resisting. . . . After several months, all toes but the big one were pressed against the inner surface. Whenever I ate fish or freshly killed meat, my feet would swell, and the pus would drip."

This was the centuries-old tradition that Gladys Aylward faced in the job the Mandarin gave her. Gladys initially resisted the assignment, but it suddenly occurred to her that travelling from village to village under the Mandarin's protection would give her the chance to tell more people about Jesus. Not only could she liberate their feet; she could liberate their souls.

According to Alan Burgess in his book *The Small Woman*, Gladys responded to the Mandarin in this way: "You must realize, Excellency, that if I accept this position I shall try to convert the people of this province to Christianity wherever I go!"

When the Mandarin fell silent, Gladys feared she had gone too far. But then he answered softly, "I care nothing for your religion or to whom you preach. This is a matter for the conscience of each individual. But it is important that you should do this work."

She did.

At first people reacted to Gladys with a nervous wariness. When people from the first village were summoned to the square, they kept their distance, both physically and psychologically. They weren't sure what to make of it all. Gladys wasn't sure what to make of it either, but she was determined to appear confident.

With a crowd behind her, Gladys marched to the nearest house, where she found a girl of about three years. "That one," she commanded, pointing at the girl. "Unbind her feet!"

To overcome her nervousness, Burgess explains, Gladys talked unceasingly while four women slowly unwrapped the bandages. With the bandages off, Gladys moved to her knees, pried the girl's toes away from the sole and massaged them. "Five little piggies all ready to go to market," smiled Gladys, and the atmosphere suddenly lightened. Tensions released. The little girl was delighted.

Women of varying ages immediately pushed forward, all of them chattering about the pain they had endured for so many years. Gladys was quickly promoted from a "foreign devil" to a person of honor.

Footbinding is a graphic illustration of how women have been subjugated. It's also a symbol of how the church in America has been similarly bound.

In the United States, churches are bound financially. This may seem strange in a country with so much money, but it's true. Instead of channeling our funds outwardly for the work of missionaries such as Gladys, we turn much of it inward and spend it on ourselves. The result is the same as that of a Chinese woman whose toes are pulled inward. The church becomes handicapped.

Certainly there are good uses for money within our churches. But an incredible amount of our resources is wrapped up in the tradition of binding ourselves in debt to make capital improvements. New buildings. New organs. New carpeting. New air conditioning.

In 1988, John and Sylvia Ronsvalle of empty tomb, inc. in Champaign, Illinois, documented the giving habits of members of thirty-one denominations. From 1968 to 1985, the after-tax, per capita income of Americans increased, even taking inflation into consideration, but the percentage Christians gave to churches decreased.

To be exact, Americans saw their after-tax income increase by an average of $2,511 per person between 1968 and 1985. But giving in the thirty-one denominations increased by only $49 per person.

Sadder yet, the Ronsvalles found that churches were giving much less to outside ministries. In fact, after taking inflation into consideration, they found virtually no increase in the amount of money going to outside efforts.

In 1990, the Ronsvalles updated their study for twenty-six of the denominations. They found that the percentage of income given to churches continued to decline and so did the percentage of giving to outside ministries.

When the Japanese invaded China in 1941, Gladys Aylward helped more than one hundred children escape in a treacherous journey through the mountains. They made the journey on foot. Unbound feet.

Unbound feet can travel incredible distances and do amazing things, but an unbound church can do even more.

REAL LIFE

A Mind-Boggling Puzzle for "Superior" People

Quiz time. Read the following two stories and then figure out how they relate to each other.

True Story #1

Dave and Leanne, both youth pastors, waited at their church. The van was filled with gas, ready to carry six high school students to a Baptist Youth Convention in Chicago.

But not everything was ready. There were no kids. Nobody had shown up, and it was time to leave. Dave telephoned one of the students.

"Uh, sorry, Dave," said the embarrassed voice on the other end of the line. "I gotta help my Dad with chores on the farm. I can't go."

Five kids were now going to the youth convention in Chicago.

Dave called another high schooler.

"Sorry, but I can't go," said the next voice. "I'm really sorry."

Correction: Four kids were going to the Baptist Youth Convention.

Dave called again.

Three kids were going.

Dave called again.

Two kids were going.

Dave called again.

One kid was going to the Baptist Youth Convention.

Ironically, the five kids who backed out at the last minute were all children of church members. The one who actually showed up was not part of the church. He was a friend of one of the other kids.

When Dave and Leanne returned from the weekend convention, Dave had an encounter with a deacon. The deacon gave Dave an earful.

"You took *one* kid to a convention!?" the deacon fumed. "That's not a productive use of your time! That's not good business!"

What was even more horrifying to the deacon was that the kid wasn't a member of their church. It was bad enough wasting time on one kid. But to waste it on SOMEONE WHO DIDN'T GO TO THEIR CHURCH! Unbelievable!

"We're not paying you to work with kids from other churches!" exclaimed the deacon.

Dave's response was an easy one. He told the deacon that "the one kid" became a Christian on the trip.

The deacon dropped the subject, but Dave could tell he still was not convinced that church resources had been used wisely.

The kid went on to become an associate pastor in a Baptist church.

True Story #2

Believe it or not, what I am about to tell you really happened in America. In Kansas, of all places. Home of Toto and Dorothy. Home of the Fitter Families Contest.

The what?

Let me explain.

In the 1920s, state fairs in Kansas featured more than just cows and pigs. In addition to livestock, the fairgrounds had "human stock" sections in which families were judged. In a typical Fitter Families Contest, all members of a family had a physical exam, underwent psychiatric assessment, and took an intelligence test. The most well-bred humans were called "Grade-A Individuals" and went home with a trophy.

As one contest brochure explained, "The time has come when the

science of human husbandry must be developed based on the principles now followed by scientific agriculture, if the better elements of our
civilization are to dominate or even survive."

If this sounds more bizarre than Munchkin land, welcome to the
world of eugenics. The eugenics movement, a potent force before
World War II, was based on the principle that sound breeding and
genetic research could produce a superrace.

Eugenicists worked like mad trying to figure out ways to get "superior" people to breed and to discourage "inferior" people from having
babies. According to Jeremy Rifkin's book *Who Should Play God?* a 1907

law in Indiana called for "mandatory sterilization of confirmed criminals, idiots, imbeciles, and others in state institutions when approved
by a board of experts." (I'm surprised the Indiana legislature passed
this; the phrase "idiots in state institutions" could have been interpre-
ted to mean them.)

The eugenics movement became so powerful that even President
Teddy Roosevelt is reported to have said, "Criminals should be sterilized
and feebleminded persons forbidden to leave offspring behind them. . . .
The emphasis should be laid on getting desirable people to breed."

The eugenics movement was dealt a major blow when Nazi Ger-
many took its ideas to the most brutal extreme. Nevertheless, many
people today still try to resurrect its principles. For instance, a Nobel
Prize winner was quoted as saying, "No newborn infant should be
declared human until it has passed certain tests regarding its genetic
endowment, and . . . if it fails these tests it forfeits the right to live."

A prominent law professor reportedly suggested that couples who
are genetically superior should be given more tax deductions for having children than those who are genetically inferior. Others have suggested that people be allowed to reproduce only if they have a license
(which is given to genetically favorable people).

Quiz Answer

So how do these two stories relate?

They both have to do with efficiency. In fact, the eugenics movement was a spin-off of the efficiency movement, which said that we
should make the best, most efficient use of our natural resources. With
eugenics, leaders tried to apply efficiency to *people* rather than natural
resources.

When you're dealing with people, however, efficiency is a lousy
goal. It should not be the standard for physical reproduction or for spiritual regeneration.

Unfortunately, the deacon in Story #1 tried to convince Dave and
Leanne that their youth program should be based on some sort of

spiritual eugenics. He tried to make efficiency the driving force behind their ministry. He tried to convince Dave that ministering to one kid wasn't an efficient use of time.

But an obsession with numbers isn't the only way church programs fall into the efficiency trap. In church, as in all areas of life, it's much easier to focus on the "efficient" people. People with obvious talents. People who are easy to get along with. People who won't waste our time by constantly talking about their problems.

Yes, it's more efficient to focus programs and energy on people who have it all together. But it's a lot less loving.

God doesn't treat us efficiently; he loves us too much.

While writing a magazine article about the eugenics movement two years ago, I talked with Andrew Kimbrell, a lawyer with the Foundation on Economic Trends in Washington, D.C. Kimbrell said, "We don't treat anything or anybody we love on an efficiency basis. We don't determine how many hugs we are going to give our children on a minimum input/maximum output basis. I don't even treat my pet dog on an efficiency basis. It works for machines. But it doesn't work for those we love."

ORIGINS

Raised Hands. The earliest Christians didn't fold their hands during prayer. They held their hands up to heaven, palms out, to catch blessings from God. Christians also were known to fold their hands across their chest with their wrists crossing above the heart.

Folding Hands in Prayer. There are numerous explanations for how the tradition of folding hands in prayer started. One of the most interesting ideas has to do with the practice of shackling prisoners.

Think about it. When a prisoner's hands are shackled, or tied, they are often held in front, as if in prayer. In fact, whenever a Roman wanted to surrender and avoid getting killed, he clasped his hands in front of him—as if they were shackled.

Folded hands became a symbol of surrender to God.

The Sign of the Cross. To make the sign of the cross, Christians first touch their forehead, then their chest, then one shoulder, then the other. The early Christians used it is as a signal to identify themselves to one another as believers during the time of Roman persecution.

Christians use three fingers to make the sign of the cross to symbolize the Father, Son, and Holy Spirit. The other two fingers represent the two natures of Jesus—fully man and fully God.

Bible Verses and Chapters. The Bible was not divided into chapters until 1226 when Stephen Langton, a professor at the University of Paris, broke it into chapters to improve readability. In 1551, Robert Stephen, a printer, added verse numbers, using a system developed by Santos Pagnini in 1528.

Amen. One of the most common ways to infiltrate pagan cultures has been to change the meaning of their words. The Hebrews did this with the Egyptian word *Amun*. The chief god of the Egyptians was "Amun," or "the hidden one."

The Hebrews gave new meaning to this pagan word by transforming "Amun" to "Amen." They ended speeches and sermons with "Amen," which means "so it is." It emphasized that they were telling the truth.

THE **SEVENTH** DAY

Everyone Rested, Except the Minister and Every Sunday School Teacher on Earth

By the seventh day God had finished the work he had been doing; so on the seventh day he rested from all his work. And God blessed the seventh day and made it holy, because on it he rested from all the work of creating that he had done.

GENESIS 2:2–3

Technically, Sunday is the first day of the week, not the seventh. But since it is the day of rest, it *feels* more like the last day. So let's examine its role as the Christian Sabbath—a time when families across the land come together. A time for fellowship, fun, and refreshment. A time when families ask the all-important question, "Which family member will lose his or her cool first during the mad rush to leave the house for church?"

Sunday also is a time when ministers ask themselves such questions as, "How can I signal that the service is about to begin so everyone will stop chattering and moving about?"

The traditional way to get a congregation settled down is to play organ music. This has been effective for generations. But today's young adults were raised on rock and roll. When music starts, it's not a signal to *stop* talking; it's a signal to start talking LOUDER!! Remember, these young adults have spent many hours at parties with the stereo turned up full volume, holding conversations like this:

Marilyn: I LIKE YOUR SHIRT!!!!!

Joe: WHAT?!!!!!!!!

Marilyn: THREE O'CLOCK!!!!!!!

Joe: NO, I LEFT IT AT HOME!!!!!

Marilyn: WHAT?!!!!

Joe: THAT'S DEFINITELY TRUE!!!!!!

Marilyn: OKAY!!!

Seating Latecomers

Once the service gets underway, there is yet another predicament—seating latecomers. Usually this is done by ushers who try to get the people settled quietly so that nobody notices.

Herein lies the problem. If you allow latecomers to go unnoticed, they will never learn to be on time. What they need is public ridicule and scorn. Therefore, to discourage tardiness, have the ushers escort them through a secret tunnel underneath the church that opens directly in front of the pulpit in full view of everyone.

Keep a supply of last week's bulletins in the front pews for people to wad up and throw at chronic latecomers as they exit the tunnel.

Children in Church

Taking children to church is not much different from taking them across country in a Chevette. The length of time is a little different, but the space involved is about the same.

On car rides, children are programmed to ask, "Are we there yet?" five minutes after leaving the driveway and every five minutes thereafter. In church they ask, "Is it over yet?" before the organ prelude is even completed. On long car rides and in church, parents spend half of

their time dumping toys and art supplies on kids' laps to keep them occupied. The rest of the time they spend trying to stop boundary disputes.

Come to think of it, the only difference between taking children to church and taking them on a cross-country vacation is that in a car parents have the freedom to shout. In church, they have to do all of their discipline quietly enough to avoid excommunication.

There is, however, one perfect, flawless, and unbelievably effective way to get kids to quiet down in church. The only trouble is that it will only work on *someone else's* kids.

Step 1: Glance very, very quickly in the child's direction to send a subtle message that you're bothered. (Important: This signal is meant for the child's parents, not for the child. If a child sees that you are irritated, the noise level will probably double.) If this signal doesn't work, move to step two.

Step 2: Stare in the child's direction and hold that stare for approximately three seconds.

Step 3: Glare at the child for ten seconds, then frown for five seconds.

Step 4: Hand the child a toy coated with axle grease. Within ten seconds, the parents will rush the child to the bathroom, where they will spend the rest of the service cleaning up.

This method is guaranteed to work for one year or 104 sermons, whichever comes first.

Music

One of the universal mysteries of the faith is how conflict can center on such a positive, upbeat portion of a service as music. In every church, some people want traditional hymns while others prefer worship choruses. Some people want classical music, while others wouldn't mind if the pastor roller-skated backwards down the aisle with a boom box on his shoulder playing reggae music.

And it's getting even more complicated because many churches today are squabbling over whether some hymns are sexist, war-like, or just plain confusing.

What's stranger, the Church of Perpetual Chauvinism in Flittle, New York, continues to make its hymns *more* sexist. Sylvia Oppenheim, president of the National Association of Women Who Occasionally Get to Appear With Fifty-Two Male Speakers at Large Christian Conferences, is outraged. She is especially irked that this New York church portrays wives as nags by singing "Good Christian Men Rejoice, Your Wife Just Lost Her Voice!"

To emphasize their manhood, the church elders have even composed a hymn in praise of chest hair: "God Rest Ye, Hairy Gentlemen." Also in the works are "Hark, the Macho Angels Sing" and its sequel, "Yo! the Macho Angels Sing."

The Offering

If the love of money is the root of all evil, how can you take an offering in a way that doesn't make you look like a money-grubbing charlatan? Here are several options.

Option 1: Pass offering plates down the aisle. Drawback: People will feel pressured to give.

Option 2: Leave baskets in the back of the church so people can give if they feel led. Drawback: People will forget the baskets are there.

Option 3: Leave baskets in the back of the church but have people stationed next to them who constantly clear their throats and motion with their heads in the direction of the baskets.

Altar Calls

Altar calls are an opportunity at the end of the service for people to go to the front of the church and dedicate their lives to Christ. This is great. The problem comes when the minister feels that if nobody comes forward he has failed.

In such cases, certain ministers will fall back on the old rededication strategy. They ask Christians who want to recommit their lives to Christ to step forward. This too is fine and good, as long as the minister doesn't do it just to get somebody to come forward.

If nobody comes in this second phase, things can get really uncomfortable. That's when a minister may resort to this:

Minister: Will anybody who recommitted their lives in the last five years please come forward?

(Five minutes pass. Nobody moves.)

Minister: Uh . . . Will anybody who knows anybody who was once *thinking* about recommitting their lives please step forward?

(Four minutes pass. Nobody moves.)

Minister: OK, then will anybody who knows the definition of the word "recommitment" please step forward?

(Three minutes pass. Nobody moves.)

Minister: Will anybody who doesn't want their tires deflated in the parking lot by the Bluto brothers please step forward?

(A mad rush for the altar.)

THE FIRST CHURCH OF ESPECIALLY SWELL PEOPLE, REFORMED

"The friendly church where even the pastor's wife feels accepted"

SUNDAY, JANUARY 3

*Prelude in Music** (in stereo where available)

"In-a-Gadda-Da-Vida in D Minor"
Senior Choir, Jane Lilly on violin, Jack Lilly on largemouth bass

*Scripture Reading***

Exodus 16:36. "An omer is one-tenth of an ephah."

*The Three Stooges Kiss of Peace****

Turn to your neighbor and say "Nyuk, nyuk, nyuk, nyuk." Then bonk them over the head, bark like a dog, go "Woo-woo-woo-woo-woo," and pretend to poke them in the eyes.

*The Offering*****

All churchgoers wearing pants are asked to stand on their heads while ushers wait for loose change to fall on the carpet.

*The Sermon******

Rev. Bobo Hixson forgot his sermon notes today, so he is going to lip-synch to a Tony Campolo tape.

*Rebuttal to Last Week's Sermon*******

Title: "If Evil Were a Substance, Would It Look Like Creamed Peas or Brussels Sprouts?"

---

*Stand up
**Sit down
***Fight, fight, fight!
****Latecomers will be seated
*****Latecomers will be shot
******Don't bother listening to this

Screaming-Baby Switch

All parents holding babies are asked to switch to a new seat so the same people don't have to sit next to a crying infant all service long.

Responsive Reading

PASTOR: *Who's sitting in the pew?*
CONGREGATION: *No. Who is on first.*
PASTOR: *I don't know.*
CONGREGATION: *I-Don't-Know is in the nursery.*
PASTOR: *What?*
CONGREGATION: *No. What is in the foyer.*
PASTOR: *I don't know.*
CONGREGATION: *And also with you.*

Personal Sharing

Impersonal Sharing

The Final Greeting

Members are asked to greet one another either by giving the "high-five" or by running across the room, affectionately bumping heads together, and then doing an end-zone dance.

Final Hymn

Lyrics to this hymn were changed in honor of "Bodybuilding Sunday," which is being observed today. Please sing the following:

> *A mighty fitness is my bod, a bulwark never spraining.*
> *My muscles they, amid the gleam,*
> > *look gross when they are straining.*
> *Oh, give me mirrors galore; my biceps I adore;*
> *My veins stick out six feet; I look like groc'ry meat.*
> *On earth I have no equal.*

The Dismissal

PASTOR: *Get lost, you knuckleheads.*
CONGREGATION: *See you later, alligator.*

Today's Helpers

Organist: Jean Osmand

Person who turns sheet music pages for the organist while she plays: Linda Omar

Manicurist who does the organist's nails while she plays: Karen Omar

Big burley men who fan the organist with palm branches while she plays: Joe-Joe Omar, Kevin "The Beef" Omar

Greeters: Larry and Jean Osmand at the front doors, Tom and Jennifer Brock at the back doors, Marge and Bud Kelso on the roof (to greet parachutists)

Today's Adult Bible Studies

"Holistic Bowling: Is It a Cult?" taught by Jenny Perkins

"Translating the Old Testament Into Whale Calls" taught by Professor Simon Yates

"Did the Pharaoh Use the Plagues As a Tax Write-off?" taught by Myra Caulking, Certified Public Accountant

Today's Activities

You are cordially invited to a special ceremony to dedicate Russell Milhouse's new invention, the Potluck Detector. This computerized scanner can detect whether people attending potlucks have gone to a fast-food restaurant (such as Kentucky Fried Chicken) and then placed the chicken in a casserole dish to make it look home-cooked. At one o'clock this afternoon in de Farringer Hall.

Attention Men!

Next Saturday's pancake breakfast has been canceled. The three paramedics who usually pump stomachs after the meal are all on vacation.

ODD-SERVATIONS

*An Inside Look at the First Church of Especially Swell People, Reformed**

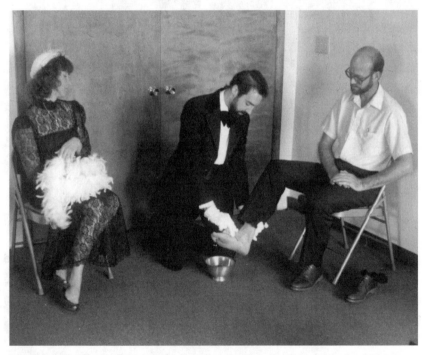

Somehow, Mrs. Olivia de Farringer has missed the point of the church's recent footwashing ceremony. However, the butler she hired to do her part in the ceremony said he was spiritually moved.

* Photos courtesy of Bud Kelso, First Church photographer.

As the Brock family prepares for church, Tom Brock wears the "Spouse-Cam"— a device that has reduced the need for marital counseling by fifty percent. This handy camcorder is worn by husbands and wives during the hectic time before church, when the entire family battles over one bathroom, when the husband tells the wife it's her turn to get the two-year-old ready, and when the wife says she's going to stay home if he dares to get in the car and start honking for her to hurry up.

With a Spouse-Cam recording every move, husbands and wives maintain remarkably good behavior, reports church librarian Trina Cartwright. She should know, because copies of all Spouse-Cam video tapes are kept in the church library.

"The new Spouse-Cam program has also increased use of the church library by three-hundred percent," says Carpenter.

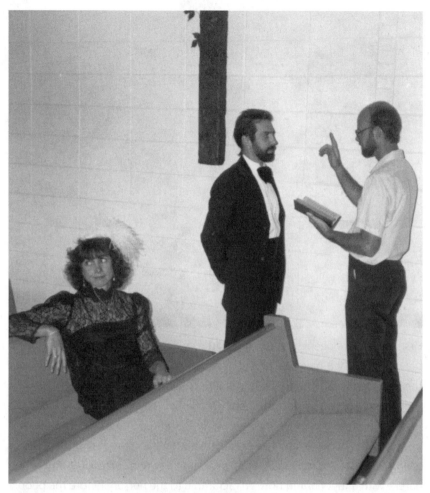

Somehow, the First Church society queen, Mrs. Olivia de Farringer, has missed the point of altar calls. However, the butler she sent to answer an altar call in her place said he was spiritually moved.

First, there were beepers, those noisy little devices that go off in the middle of prayers. Now, we have beepers that are even more offensive—but they get the job done when your baby is in the nursery.

As you know, our nursery motto is, "Babies: You bring 'em, you change 'em." Therefore, if your child creates a mess and needs a diaper change, this beeper will alert you to the need no matter where you may be. But instead of giving off a loud, obnoxious sound, it will emit a strong, obnoxious smell. Any parent with a functioning nose will scramble to the nursery before the people sitting anywhere in the vicinity smash the device into sand-sized particles.

REAL LIFE

Turtle Races: Never on Sunday

Rest is crucial for spiritual and physical health. We know it. And God knows it. That's why he created the Sabbath Day rest.

Fortunately, God *wasn't* responsible for some of the ludicrous laws we have passed in an attempt to protect the Sabbath. Here are just a few laws that were actually passed at one time or another. Some of these laws have been pulled from the books, but some remain.*

- In Slaughter, Louisiana: It's against the law to conduct turtle races on the Sabbath. What's more, turtle races can *never* be held within one hundred yards of a church.

- In Winchester, Massachusetts: Girls cannot walk a tightrope, unless the tightrope is in a church.

- In Chaseville, New York: On Sunday, it's expressly forbidden to lead a goat in front of a church "in a ridiculous fashion."

- In Leona, Kansas: On the Sabbath, firemen cannot rescue women wearing nightgowns. A woman must get dressed before she can be rescued.

- In Memphis, Tennessee: You cannot sell bologna on Sunday.

* Sources: Hyman, Dick. *The Trenton Pickle Ordinance.* Brattleboro, Vermont: The Stephen Greene Press, 1976. Hyman, Dick. *Cockeyed Americana,* Brattleboro, Vermont: The Stephen Greene Press, 1972. Pelton, Robert. "Laughable (But True) Laws Concerning the Church and Sabbath." T*he Wittenburg Door,* February–March 1986, 22–23.

- In Omaha, Nebraska: The law cracks down on anyone who sneezes or burps during church.

- In Michigan: A man can get into legal hot water if he kisses his wife on the Sabbath.

- In Garysburg, North Carolina: You cannot shoot any animals, except whales, from an airplane on the Sabbath. Also, you cannot shoot fish while church is going on.

- In Massachusetts: A law forbids the delivery of clean diapers on Sunday, even under dire circumstances.

- In Providence, Rhode Island: It's OK for a drugstore to sell toothpaste on Sunday, but it's illegal to sell toothbrushes.

- In Vermont: It's against the law for women to be out on the streets

on Sundays. However, it is permissible if the woman's husband walks twenty steps behind her and is carrying a musket.

- In Kansas: "Ring around the Rosy" is forbidden on the Sabbath. It's also against the law to eat snakes on Sunday.

- In Memphis, Tennessee: Yo-yos and Teddy Bears cannot be sold on the day of rest.

- In Georgia: A person can be charged with a misdemeanor if he shows up at church *without* his gun. Also, the gun must be loaded.

- In Cicero, Illinois: People walking down the street cannot hum on Sunday.

- In Alabama: You can be arrested for wearing a false moustache to church and causing someone to laugh.

REAL LIFE

Start the Revolution Without Me
'Cause I'm Resting

In 1792, parts of France fell under the Reign of Terror.

Religious symbols were banished from graveyards. People were encouraged to vandalize churches. Church bells were removed so people wouldn't hear something that reminded them of religion. Crosses were removed so people wouldn't see something that reminded them of religion. Street names were changed so people wouldn't read something that reminded them of religion. And priests were not allowed to wear clerical outfits that would remind people of religion.

But strangest of all, the terms B.C. and A.D. were rendered obsolete so references to times and dates would not remind people of religion.

In France, 1792 became known as Year I, the year when the French Revolution began.

Traditional months were scrapped and replaced with new months, all named after parts of nature—Mist, Frost, Snow, Wind, Seeds, etc. The days of the week were given numbers instead of names. And all saints' days and holy days were dumped.

To top it off, the Sabbath was eliminated. The seventh day of rest was replaced by a more "scientific," less religious day of rest—the *decadi,* which was observed once every ten days instead of every seven. Like the Sabbath, it was marked with special ceremonies. As you might suspect, however, these festivals were far from religious.

France at this time had a festival for just about every revolutionary cause, and one of the most notorious was the Festival of Reason. For instance, one of the festivals in Chartes was entitled "Reason Victorious over Fanaticism" and was performed in a church.

In this ceremony, a woman wearing a tricolor helmet was carried up into the air by a machine made to look like a cloud. With a spear in her hand, the woman rose up in her cloud until she came before the statue of Reason. There, she discovered a new world where Reason ruled and everyone lived in glorious harmony.

It was all a cheap substitute for the Sabbath, and like most cheap things, it didn't last long at all. Workers found it physically and emotionally draining to follow the new, secular Sabbath—once every ten days.

The Sabbath couldn't be replaced by force. But can it be replaced in more subtle ways? Has our culture done just that?

At one extreme, the Sabbath has been straight-jacketed by legalistic, ludicrous laws. I have friends who say that Sunday was the most oppressive day of the week because they weren't allowed to do anything. But have we gone to the other extreme? Have we totally lost our sense of Sabbath rest? Do we cram our Sabbath into a 45-minute church service, then race for the parking lot so we can get home to our lawn work and projects?

Going without a Sabbath day of rest is a lot like going without sleep.

In 1959 a New York disc jockey named Peter Tripp vowed to stay awake for two hundred hours in return for financial pledges. To make the spectacle more public, Tripp broadcast live from behind a window overlooking Times Square. According to Christopher Evans' account in *Landscapes of the Night,* doctors monitored Tripp's health and also made sure that he stayed awake.

During the first two days, Tripp became sluggish and stumbled over words. On the third day, he began hallucinating. He saw cobwebs on his feet and felt cobwebs brushing against his face. He also thought he was joined by a rabbit, who kept him company for a little while, and he periodically watched a troop of imaginary insects march by his equipment. But Tripp knew they were hallucinations so he wasn't too bothered.

After one hundred hours, the situation became much less amusing. Tripp started believing the hallucinations. The insects now appeared dangerous. When he went to a nearby hotel to change clothes, he opened a closet and thought it was filled with fire. His shouts set off a panic in the hotel.

What's worse, he became paranoid, believing that doctors had set the fire just to see how he would react. He thought everyone around him was hostile. When he mistook one of the doctors for an undertaker, he went screaming into the street. That's when people decided he should call it quits.

Peter Tripp took a thirteen-hour snooze. When he woke up, the hallucinations were gone, but he was mildly depressed for the next three months.

Forgetting to observe the Sabbath rest might not turn us into psychotics. But this example of sleep deprivation still serves as a good symbol of what happens to us when we deprive ourselves of the Lord's Day. The benefits of sleep parallel the benefits of Sabbath rest.

Sleep helps the brain clear out clutter, enables the body to recuperate, allows us to work out problems subconsciously, and provides a time to dream. Sabbath rest provides similar advantages for our spirits. It allow us to clear up clutter from the week and work out problems both consciously and subconsciously. It also gives us time to dream.

We were not made for sleep. But sleep was made for us. We were not made for the Sabbath. But the Sabbath was made for us. It's a gift.

ORIGINS

Sunday. For the Jews, the Sabbath falls on the last day of the week—the seventh day, when God rested after creating the world. The early Christian church changed its day of worship to Sunday in honor of the day that Jesus rose from the dead. The change also helped to set Christians apart from those of the Jewish faith.

Maundy Thursday. Maundy Thursday comes from the Latin word *mandatum*, which means "commandment." At the Last Supper, on the Thursday night before he died, Jesus gave a new commandment. He said, "A new command I give you: Love one another. As I have loved you, so you must love one another" (John 13:34). Christians celebrate this commandment on Maundy Thursday.

Good Friday. Jesus was crucified on Friday, so why call it "good?" Some say the day was named Good Friday to emphasize that good can emerge from the midst of evil. Resurrection follows death. But others say the name was just a corruption of the original name, "God's Friday."

In Durham, England, blacksmiths were once unwilling to shoe horses on Good Friday because they didn't want to use nails—the tools used to kill Jesus. Also, colonial churchgoers in America sometimes went barefoot on Good Friday. They didn't want the nails on their shoes to leave marks in the ground.

Easter. In the early church Christian leaders were concerned that Easter sometimes fell on the same day as the Jewish Passover celebration.

During the council at Nicaea in A.D. 325, the leaders decided that Easter would be celebrated on the Sunday *following* the full moon that falls on or comes right after the vernal equinox. Because Passover *coincides* with the full moon, the two holidays would never again be on the same day.

Christmas. In the early church, many people thought that celebrating birthdays was a pagan practice. So they didn't like the idea of celebrating a birthday for Jesus.

Later, however, Christians decided it was more effective to create alternatives to pagan celebrations than to eliminate or ignore them. Sometime during the fourth century they decided to celebrate Christmas on December 25—already a day of Roman celebration.

When days became short in the winter, the Romans were afraid that the earth was dying. So they celebrated the Feast of the Unconquerable Sun on December 25 in honor of the sun's return and longer days. While Romans were busy celebrating the return of their sun, a band of renegades calling themselves Christians celebrated the arrival of God's Son.

AND GOD SAW
THAT IT WAS GOOD

And the angel said to them, "Be not afraid; for behold, I bring you good news of a great joy which will come to all the people; for to you is born this day in the city of David a Savior, who is Christ the Lord. And this will be a sign for you: you will find a babe wrapped in swaddling cloths and lying in a manger."

Luke 2:10–12 RSV

It is only fitting that I end this book at the same point where it started, the same point where Christianity began. At Jesus' birth. Christmas.

About a dozen times each Christmas, I hear the words "swaddling cloths." But I have never stopped to find out what in the world a swaddling cloth really is . . . until now.

My minister, Ron Simkins, recently explained that Hebrew babies born during Jesus' day were washed, rubbed with salt, then placed on a square cloth and wrapped up. So far so good. Dr. Spock would approve (except perhaps of the salt). But then came the really unusual part. Swaddling bands were wrapped so tightly around the cloth that the child's arms were immobilized at its sides.

Evidently they believed swaddling was necessary to prevent fragile bones from breaking. So they immobilized a baby's arms for up to several months, sometimes loosening the bands during the day.

The image of Jesus' arms being tied to his sides reinforces my amazement at God's humility. As my pastor pointed out, not only was God

189

willing to come to us as a baby, not only was he willing to be born in a stable, but he was willing to submit to some very strange child-rearing techniques. He was willing to give up power, yes; but he was also willing to become totally immobilized.

Writer Philip Yancey reminds his readers that God's willingness to visit earth as a powerless baby was only *one* of his great humiliations. Another occurred when he returned to heaven and left his work in the hands of the church. As you have seen from our short review of church life, we are far from perfect. We make some awful messes. But the truly astounding thing is that God is still willing to put up with us. He's willing to let the church be his arms.

That is more than humility. That is love—pure, undiluted love.

Mike Yaconelli, a popular speaker among youth workers, uses an image that captures the essence of this love. He tells about a friend of his, a father, who followed the same ritual every evening: Go into the kitchen, get a glass from the cupboard, take out a cookie, open the refrigerator, pour milk into the glass, sit in front of the television, and watch the evening news.

One night the father broke his routine and went directly to the television. His three-year-old son, apparently noticing this change in ritual, waddled toward the kitchen. Curious as to what his son was up to, the father decided to watch what happened.

As Mike Yaconelli tells it, the little boy walked into the kitchen, pulled out a bottom drawer (which he wasn't supposed to do), stood on top of it, jumped on it, pulled himself up onto the counter, opened the cabinet door, reached in, grabbed a glass (knocking over two other glasses), pulled the glass out, set it down on the counter, hopped back down to the bottom drawer and then to the floor, walked over to where the cookies were stored, reached up, grabbed them (knocking a bunch of cookies onto the floor and sending crumbs everywhere), picked up three of the fallen cookies, put two of them back, held the other one in his hand, walked over to the refrigerator, opened the refrigerator, put everything down again, pulled out a gallon of milk (which weighed about as much as he did), pulled the lid off, poured milk all the way to the top of the glass and spilled some over the brim, picked up the cookie, picked up the glass, spilled more milk, and walked over to his dad (leaving the refrigerator door open).

"Any other time and that kid would have been in big trouble," the father said. "I would have throttled him for what he did. But as he walked to me, I recognized what he was doing. My little three-year-old boy was giving me a gift. And what else could I do but throw my arms around my son?"

Sure, we make a mess out of our churches. But God realizes that behind our strange rituals, stubbornness, in-fighting, and goofball mistakes, there lies a gift. A gift for our Father.

God understands. He knows what it's like to be human because he lived as one of us—as both child and adult. As a child, he was willing to spend a few months with his hands immobilized in swaddling bands. As an adult, he was willing to have his hands immobilized again with nails and a wooden beam.

Allowing his hands and arms to be immobilized on the cross was his way of throwing his arms around us.

ACKNOWLEDGMENTS

The Cast (in order of appearance)

The Lutheran minister: Tim Offenstein

Other people in the "Immerse Me" photo: John P. Brown, Dave Lucas, Leanne Lucas

Bob Holliman: Henry J. Seiter, Jr.

Two teenagers: Adam Fein, Brad Whetten

Shy Bible study: Francois Grobler, Kathy Kearney-Grobler, Michael J. McQueen, Gwynne McQueen, Wilmer Zehr

Sleepy minister in Pastor-Compassion, International ad: Dave Lucas

Minister with dot in front of face: Dave Lucas

Joshua Hixson: Michael Peterson

Esther Hixson: Holly S. Brown

The Extremely Reverend Bobo Hixson: Dave Lucas

Claudia Kraft: Connie Thompson

Jethro Kraft: Dave Thompson

The horse: Garrett Smith's pony, "Moose"

Person pouring water into "Mr. Baptism": John P. Brown

Person with head under "Mr. Baptism": Peter J. Woods

Trick or teachers: Jason Peterson, Michael Peterson

Person scooping green-bean casserole: Theotric L. Hunt

People praying with long poles: Theotric L. Hunt, Nancy Peterson, Karyn Simkins Hunt, Bill Sutton, Jane Sutton

Husband trying to read sports page: Judson Chubbuck

Worshippers singing to stay-at-home husband: John P. Brown, Laurel Brown, Mary Brown, Beth Chubbuck, Sharon Chubbuck, Nancy Peterson, Vivian B. Terrill

193

Static-electricity people: John P. Brown, Jerry Rabbit, Connie Thompson

The Sorta Reverend Sammy Smitt: Les Pritchard

Jean Osmand: Nancy Peterson

Nick Johnson: Seth Hutchinson

Marty Quinn: Mike Orfanedes

The headbell choir: Lenita J. Epinger, Frank C. Modica, Janet Modica, Susan M. Surbaugh

Three softball players: Frank C. Modica, Doug Peterson, Henry J. Seiter, Jr.

People with beeper: Lenita J. Epinger, Frank C. Modica, Janet Modica, David Surbaugh, Susan M. Surbaugh

Mrs. Olivia de Farringer: Vanessa J. Grant

The butler: Tony Grant

Jennifer Brock: Jane Sutton

Tom Brock: Bill Sutton

The Brock kids: Benjamin Sutton, Matthew Sutton, Zachary Sutton

Photography by Doug Peterson

Photo of the University of Illinois Assembly Hall used with permission.

Special thanks to: Nancy, Leanne, Dave, Jane, Bill, and Mike for listening to and reading lots of stuff. Also, thanks to Wilmer for his photography tips.

Last but not second-to-last, I would like to recognize the following sources of information for the "Origins" section:

Barth, Edna. *Shamrocks, Harps, and Shillelaghs: The Story of the St. Patrick's Day Symbols*. New York: The Seabury Press, 1977.

Clowney, Paul and Tessa. *Exploring Churches*. Grand Rapids, Michigan: William B. Eerdmans Publishing Company, 1982.

Del Re, Gerard and Patricia. *The Christmas Almanack*. Garden City, New York: Doubleday and Company, Inc., 1979.

Ferguson, Charles W. *A is for Advent*. Boston: Little, Brown and Company, 1968.

Green, Victor J. *Festivals and Saints Days: A Calendar of Festivals for School and Home*. Poole, England: Blandford Press, 1978.

Joseph, Robert. *The Christmas Book*. New York: McAfee Books, 1978.

McSpadden, J. Walker. *The Book of Holidays*. New York: Thomas Y. Crowell Company, 1958.

McCollister, John C. *The Christian Book of Why*. Middle Village, New York: Jonathan David Publishers, Inc., 1983.

Mead, Frank S. *Handbook of Denominations in the United States*. Revised by Samuel S. Hill. New Eighth Edition. Nashville: Abingdon Press, 1985.

Panati, Charles. *Extraordinary Origins of Everyday Things*. New York: Harper & Row, 1987.

Potter, Charles Francis. *The Faiths Men Live By*. New York: Prentice-Hall, Inc., 1954.

Rifkin, Jeremy. *Time Wars: The Primary Conflict in Human History*. New York: Henry Holt and Company, 1987.

Wallechinsky, David, and Irving Wallace. *The People's Almanac*. Garden City, New York: Doubleday and Company, Inc., 1975.